STUDIES IN THE PHONOLOGY OF
COLLOQUIAL ENGLISH

Studies in the Phonology of Colloquial English

K.R. LODGE

CROOM HELM
London & Sydney

© 1984 K.R. Lodge
Croom Helm Ltd, Provident House, Burrell Row,
Beckenham, Kent BR3 1AT
Croom Helm Australia Pty Ltd, GPO Box 5097,
Sydney, NSW 2001, Australia

British Library Cataloguing in Publication Data

Lodge, Ken
    Studies in the phonology of colloquial
    English.
    1. English language – Conversations and
    phrase books
    2. English language – Slang
    I. Title
    427   PE3711
    ISBN 0-7099-1631-0

Printed in Great Britain by
Biddles Ltd, Guildford, Surrey

CONTENTS

ACKNOWLEDGEMENTS

My grateful thanks are due to my nine anonymous informants, who agreed to be recorded; also to Sylvia Mann and Veronica Du Feu who assisted in two of the recordings. I would also like to thank Jacques Durand, Steve Pulman and Peter Trudgill for their helpful comments on and discussion of various parts of the book. The book would never have reached its final form, had it not been for the untiring and patient efforts of Moira Eagling, who typed the whole thing with great enthusiasm and consistency. Any faults in the end-product are nevertheless my responsibility. Finally, I am most grateful to Tim Hardwick , of Croom Helm, for keeping the book going in the right direction; I hope his patience is rewarded in this offering.

To Jackie

INTRODUCTION

This book has two main aims: one, to try to determine
how best to account for both the differences and the
similarities of phonological variation in British
English within the general framework of native
speaker competence; two, to establish a relatively
small set of phonological processes to relate different styles of speech within one variety. To these
ends I have investigated the speech of a small number
of informants from disparate parts of Britain, vary-
ing in age and sex. This apparently haphazard choice
of informants was determined by two considerations:
geographical distance, to ensure that the speech
would show up significant differences, and my ability
to record informants in as natural a situation as
possible, given the constraints of recording on tape.
To make this most likely, I arranged recording
sessions either with people who knew me well, or
involved a good friend of my informant. The technique in the recording sessions was one of inducing
natural conversation rather than using a question-
and-answer interview structure.
    Since I wanted to examine variation in English
colloquial speech, the accents chosen were ones which,
at least *prima facie*, were not in close contact with
one another, and were drawn from different social
backgrounds, both urban and rural. Since too my main
interest is phonological, rather than sociolinguistic,
I have not tried to give comprehensive pictures of
the social stratification at each of my chosen
localities (as is the case, for example, in Trudgill's
study of Norwich, 1974). Nor is it my intention to
present representative sketches of all possible
varieties of English (as in the case of Wells, 1982).
The spread of informants is simply to ensure varia-
bility in speech. Although I wish to stress the
phonological aims of this book, I shall nonetheless

consider certain problems of variety from a social point of view later in the Introduction. The decision to investigate natural colloquial language also has two concerns underlying it. If linguists are attempting to establish a model of native speaker competence which is concerned with the regular patterns of speech, then it is only reasonable to test hypotheses on all regular patternings in all types of speech. The emphasis has for a long time been on word- and/or morpheme-based patterns (as exemplified by the pregenerative structuralists, e.g. Hockett, 1958, and Trager and Smith, 1951, and by the dominant TG approach of Chomsky and Halle, 1968), and even those interested in different tempi tend to use one- or two-word examples (e.g. Stampe, 1979). More thorough investigation of what Dressler (1975) calls "allegro rules" is necessary to add to the battery of word-based data already available. This book is a contribution to the presentation and discussion of conversation-based data in the expansion of the model of native speaker competence. It is for this reason, too, that I have presented extracts from my recorded material in fairly narrow transcription, so that any claims I make can be checked by the reader directly (given that my transcription is a reliable representation of the speech).

The second consideration follows from the first: do the phonological processes which are well described in the word-based analyses also occur in continuous conversation? Indeed, to put the question in a more extreme form, are word-boundaries relevant in rapid colloquial speech, where they quite clearly undergo considerable alteration (see, for example, Zwicky's brief discussion of Welsh, 1972)? We need to discover whether or not the phonological processes discernible in rapid speech are fundamentally different from those of slow, careful speech. The main difference may be that in slow speech any processes that occur are for the most part obligatory, whereas in rapid speech they are optional. For example, in all varieties of English *pleasure*, which, we will assume, has an underlying /-zj-/, undergoes a "palatalization" process so that it is pronounced with a medial [ʒ]. On the other hand, *as you* in rapid speech can be pronounced either [əz jə] or [əʒə], although the latter is more likely. This means that we shall have to differentiate between instances where a rule is applied obligatorily and instances where the same rule is applied optionally. This is a topic to which I shall return in the final chapter.

THE TERM "PHONOLOGY"
As can be seen from what has already been said, my
general approach to phonology is "generative", that is
to say, I am concerned with capturing (part of) the
tacit knowledge of the various informants I have recorded with regard to their phonological systems. The
knowledge of each idealized speaker/hearer is not necessarily represented by something that resembles formal
standard spoken English. I shall discuss the details
of the phonological component in the last chapter, when
I try to formulate the processes in rule form, but some
general considerations can usefully be dealt with here.
    For the basic element of phonological description,
I shall use the segment without entering into any discussion of other possible alternatives (e.g. the
undoubted syntagmatic or "prosodic" nature of certain
features of speech, as discussed by Lyons, 1962; Palmer,
1970; Hyman, 1975: 233-38; Goldsmith, 1976a & b; Liber-
mann and Prince, 1977, and others); nor shall I pursue
here the notion that segments can be hierarchically
modelled, as proposed by dependency phonology (see
Anderson and Jones, 1977; Anderson and Ewen, 1980;
Ewen, 1980; Lodge, 1981; Anderson, ms). However, in
the final chapter I shall consider certain phenomena
which suggest that some form of non-linear approach to
phonology is appropriate. Throughout the book I shall
work with the notion of phonetically based phonological
processes as a basic feature of phonological systems
(cf. Stampe, 1979). I shall discuss the most common
of these in British English in the next section.
    Since my main interest is in the phonetically
motivated processes, I shall not be concerned with
the phonological aspects of morphological alternations of the *serene - serenity* or *electric - elec-
tricity* type (cf. Chomsky and Halle, 1968; Fudge,
1969b). However, since this is an important theoretical issue, a brief discussion of it is in order
here. In the model proposed in SPE the lexical
entries are all morphemes with a single specification
of features from which all alternant surface realizations are derived by rules. (These lexical entries
are also fully specified in terms of features at the
systematic phonemic level, a point I shall return to
in the final chapter.) A considerable amount of the
argument in favour of this approach revolves round
the Latinate vocabulary of English (*serene - serenity*,
etc.), but words which enter into other alternations,
such as *take - took*, and those which have no alternations, e.g. *fade*, are treated in the same way.
Thus, *sane*, *take* and *fade* all have underlying /æ/ as
their vowel in the lexical entries. There are two
claims made by this approach which need particular

mention: one, that these vowel alternations are part
of a native English speaker's competence, and two,
they should be handled by phonological process rules.
The first claim is difficult to prove or disprove in
relation to all speakers of English. It is no doubt
true that educated people, who come into contact with
Latinate vocabulary a great deal, would consider
these alternations to be a productive part of their
linguistic system. If they came across a Latinate
word previously unknown to them, or were given a
made-up one, e.g. *oblatile*, they would be able to
provide the appropriate alternant(s), e.g. *oblatility*,
in this case with the alternation [aɪ] - [ɪ], as in
divine - *divinity*. However, it is much more difficult
to make claims of this sort for less sophisticated
speakers of English, who may well come across such
items of vocabulary only rarely. For them such words
do not form a substantial part of their lexicon, and
may have been learnt piecemeal([1]).

The second claim has been argued about since SPE,
and is related to the problem of abstractness of
phonological representations. Tiersma (1983) gives
a number of arguments against a solely morpheme-based
model of the lexicon. Although he uses rather more
straightforward material from Frisian, in that it can
be more easily demonstrated that the alternations in
question are non-productive and becoming fossilized,
his arguments can be applied to the Latinate vocabulary of English. One argument he puts forward is
that each member of the alternating pairs is distinctive elsewhere in the lexicon (1983: 71). This
certainly applies to the English forms too: *fade/fed*,
reed/red, *fine/fin*. However, since the biuniqueness
condition is demonstrably unhelpful in making phonological statements (cf. Hyman, 1975: 68-69 and 90-91),
this argument can only be used against identifying
all occurrences of an alternating pair with the same
underlying element, whether there are any alternations
or not. That is to say, the [ɪ] in the stressed
syllable of *divinity* can be derived from /aɪ/ because
of the alternation involved, but the [ɪ] of *fin* is a
distinct unit, /ɪ/. If the /aɪ/ of *fine* is associated
with that of *divinity*, there is still no loss of
distinction between the alternating and the non-alter-
nating types, because *fine* does not occur in contexts
where trisyllabic laxing can take place. As far as
English is concerned, the arguments against the SPE
treatment of such forms must be psychological, rather
than phonetic and distributional. Since this is
outside the scope of this book, I shall not pursue
it further, but an investigation of how children cope

4

with the acquisition of such alternations and tests of the sort outlined in footnote 1 would help to provide an answer ([2]). In terms of the interests and aims of this particular book, it is quite clear that the accents of English under discussion need all the underlying elements involved in the Latinate alternations ([3]), and that they are related morphologically in certain instances. Exactly how this should be incorporated into the grammar can be left for separate investigation. In the phonological discussions I have avoided both the extreme positions of, on the one hand, abstractness (cf. Fudge, 1967, 1969a & 1969b; Trudgill, 1974), where the underlying elements have no phonetic values, and, on the other hand, concreteness (cf. Hooper, 1976), where abstraction of any kind from the surface data is severely restricted. (See Dresher, 1981, for discussion; see also Kiparsky, 1968.)

THE PHONOLOGICAL PROCESSES
I am assuming that English is subject to a number of widespread phonological processes. Many of these have been recurrent throughout its history and some have been continuing for a century or more. (It may share them with other languages, too, but that is not the concern of the present book; on linguistic processes in general, see Aitchison, 1981; on phonological processes, both synchronic and diachronic, see especially, Stampe, 1979, and Anderson and Ewen, 1980.) However, these processes are not distributed uniformly throughout the different accents of English, and I hope to show how the different distribution of the processes helps to distinguish between the different accents. For example, intervocalic voicing of voiceless stops is a widespread feature of English phonology: it is a recurrent feature of the Peasmarsh accent (see Chapter 3), but it is not found at all in the speech of the Stockport informants (see Chapter 1). Phonological processes are not obligatory but are normal, especially in the type of English under consideration, colloquial conversation. A process relates two or more alternant forms (which may occur in different styles, e.g. colloquial versus formal); if there is no alternation, then no process applies, as far as the synchronic system is concerned. For example, in colloquial RP consonantal harmony and cluster simplification apply to nasal + alveolar stop + C sequences as in *sand-castle*. These forms are related to the careful, formal style of pronunciation, giving three possible pronunciations:

[sandkɑsl], [saŋgkɑsl] and [saŋkɑsl]. On the other
hand, with a word such as *handkerchief* no such alternant pronunciations exist: [haŋkətʃijf] is the only
one possible. In this case the process does not
apply, even though from a diachronic point of view
it did at some earlier period. Consequently, for
this word there is no underlying form: */handkətʃijf/.
The same applies *mutatis mutandis* to the /t/ in, on
the one hand, the variant pronunciations of *last news*
with and without a [t], and, on the other, words such
as *listen* and *glisten* with no alternative pronunciations.

I shall give a general description of the most
common processes here, and give further details in
the individual chapters, where I shall also introduce
a few minor ones as necessary. In the final chapter
I shall give formalized versions of the rules involved.

(i) *Lenition*
The general nature of lenition is discussed by Hyman
(1975: 164-69), Hooper (1976), Foley (1970), and
Anderson and Jones (1977), all from somewhat different
points of view. Anderson and Ewen (1980: 28) present
the following schema, which I have adapted here by
using traditional articulatory categories:

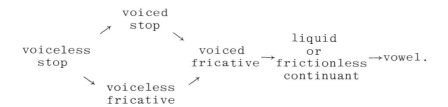

The direction of lenition is from left to right; a
sound undergoing lenition will not necessarily go
through the whole process; that is, a voiceless stop
may become a voiced stop and go no further, as in
Peasmarsh [bɑdm̩] *bottom* (line 18), or a sound further
along the chain, not itself a product of lenition,
may be subject to the next step of the process, as
when a liquid becomes a vowel in Shepherd's Bush
[stɑɪö] *style* (line 5). Voiceless stops may become
voiced stops, as in the Peasmarsh example above, or
they may become voiceless fricatives, as in Stockport
[peɪɸo] *people* (line 13). The usual environment for
lenition to take place is intervocalically.

(ii) *Harmony*
This is a more general term than the usual one,
"assimilation". Certain features of two or more
segments, either consonantal or vocalic, harmonize,
i.e. are the same in each segment. This can apply
to both contiguous and non-contiguous segments (see
Stampe, 1979: 76, and Lodge, 1983, for a discussion
of this phenomenon with reference to child language
as well). Vowel harmony is well exemplified by
Turkish (Lyons, 1962, and Hyman, 1975: 182), but does
not occur in the varieties of English presented here.
Consonantal harmony, of which there are several types
in British English, is usually called assimilation
and not given the same phonological status as vowel
harmony (cf. Gimson's discussion of English, 1962:
270-73), or it is applied to child language (cf.
Vihman, 1978). (There are also suggestions that
vowels in VCV structures harmonize generally; see
Hardcastle, 1981: 55-56.) However, there is no
reason to assume that any of these types of harmony
are not basically the same phenomenon from a phonetic
point of view. They can all come under the general
heading of ease of articulation and seem to serve the
same purpose. Whether segments intervene between the
two harmonized segments or not, does not make any
difference. In fact, Stampe (1979: 76) claims that
there is no such thing as non-contiguous harmony,
since the features in question continue through the
intervening segments as well (cf. also Lodge, 1983,
for a discussion of retroflexion in one instance of
somebody as pronounced by a 3¾-year-old Stockport
boy).
   The features that harmonize may be manner of
articulation, place of articulation, voice, tongue
height; in fact, any feature can harmonize. The
most common instances of harmony in English are those
of place, e.g.

   [tɛm mene?] *ten-minute* Stockport (18)

   [k'ɑːmp bɪ] *can't be* Shepherd's Bush (27)

   [əm bæk] *and back* Peasmarsh (52),

the most widespread applying to the underlying
alveolars and dentals, even in RP (cf. Gimson, loc.
cit.). The syllabic alveolar nasal harmonizes, sometimes to the preceding consonant, sometimes to the
following one, e.g.

   [ʋɛkŋ̩] *reckon* Stockport (17)

   [ɐplek'ɛeʃŋ̩ fɑm] *application form* Stockport (9).

The so-called velars, /k/ and /g/, harmonize with the following vowel, giving a range of realizations from palatal to velar, and even uvular for some speakers before [ɔː]-type vowels. I have not indicated this in the transcriptions, as it applies to all the accents under consideration (and probably all accents of English). The labials can also harmonize, but the range is only bilabial to labiodental. This is most common in the one Stockport informant, Y, e.g.

[geβ me] *give me* (9).

Another common harmony of place in English is what we might call palatalization, that is the change of /t d s z/ to a palato-alveolar in front of /j/, e.g.

[ɔːwɪʒ jɒus] *always used* Shepherd's Bush (1)

[pɹæpʃ jɒud] *perhaps you'd* Peasmarsh (53).

This is a process which has been going on for some considerable time in all types of English; some words have finished the process, as witnessed by those words with only one pronunciation with a palatal articulation, e.g. *nature*, *sugar*; others show fluctuation between two possible pronunciations, e.g. *issue* with [-sj-] or [-ʃ-]. (Note that a few words have avoided the process by dropping the palatal articulation; these words have alternative pronunciations with a non-harmonized alveolar followed by the palatal, or with no palatal at all, e.g. *suit* with [sj-] or [s-].) For the purposes of this book I am particularly interested in those cases where there are environmentally conditioned variants, in particular across word-boundaries.

Harmony of manner is less frequent, but applies most commonly to /ð/. In some speakers it applies to other sounds as well. E.g.

[an̥ n̥ə] *on the* Stockport (26)

[wɛɫ lɪ] *Well the* Shepherd's Bush (7)

[ɪn̥ n̥æʔ] *in that* Peasmarsh (34)

[əȷ̃ jə] *and you're* Stockport (25) (+ place harmony)

[dʒaβ ðɛ̃] *job then* Stockport (6)

[dɛʊ ʋof] *dead rough* Stockport (62) (+ place harmony)

In the case of /ð/ the harmony is left-to-right, rather than the more usual right-to-left.

Voice harmony is, of course, well known in English morphology, as in the formation of noun plurals, the 3rd person singular of the general tense and the past

8

tense, and in this all the accents under discussion
are alike. Otherwise, it is only sporadic, as in
[pɛɪvmənᵈ] *pavement* Shepherd's Bush (28).
(It is also found in West Yorkshire speakers, as in
[bratfəd] *Bradford*, cf. Hughes and Trudgill, 1979: 58;
Wells, 1982: 367.) We may note here that one of the
alternative first stages of lenition could be interpreted as voice harmony, that is between two voiced
sounds the voicing continues through what would otherwise be a voiceless stop, as in

[bəd ɪts] *but it's* Peasmarsh (18)

[bɑdm̩] *bottom* Peasmarsh (13)

[dæɔn də] *down to* Peasmarsh (16).

(iii) *Consonant cluster simplification (CCS)*
In many contexts three (or more) consonants in series
are reduced in number. The deleted consonants are
usually stops (oral and nasal), though other sounds
are also sometimes involved, details of which I shall
give in the individual chapters. Consider the following examples:

[ʔtʃɛndʒ æ̃e̤] *changed my* Stockport (31)

[kɛπ ŋe] *kept my* Stockport (57) (+ labiodental
harmony)

[mʌɔs weɪkes lekɬ] *most weakest little* Stockport(62)

[fæɔn nɛm] *found them* Stockport (75)

[spoːs ʔ beɪ] *supposed to be* Stockport (85)

[sɛɸ ʔaʔ] *except that* Stockport (2)

[dʒos stɑk] *just stock* Stockport (21)

[dʒos ʋaeʔ] *just right* Stockport (23)

[seɪm tə] *seemed to* Stockport (48)

[dʒʌs kɔdn̩ʔ] *just couldn't* Shepherd's Bush (4)

[sɹim tə] *seemed to* Shepherd's Bush (8)

[ən̩ ŋæʔs] *and that's* Shepherd's Bush (15)

[lɔʔ sʌmθɪŋʔ] *looked something* Shepherd's Bush (48)

[paɔnz daɔn] *pounds down* Shepherd's Bush (51)

[nɛks wɪik] *next week* Shepherd's Bush (55)

[feɹs weɹɬd] *First World* Peasmarsh (25)

[dʒəs lɛf tə] *just left to* Peasmarsh (38)

[ʌɔɫ mæːn] *old man* Peasmarsh (40)

[spɛʃɫess] *specialists* Stockport (77)

[fɹɛn̥z] *friends* Edinburgh (91).

All the above are examples of /t/ and /d/ in the
context: C___+C, where + = morpheme boundary, and
the first consonant has the same voice feature as
/t/ or /d/ (⁴). This means that /t/ after voiced
sounds is not deleted. /k/ is also deleted under
the same conditions, e.g. [aːst] *asked* Coventry (69).
(/p/ may do, as well, but there are no examples in
the recorded material, cf. Lodge, 1981: 35.)
    The nasal /n/ is treated differently according
to the following sound and from locality to locality.
For example, in Stockport it is either deleted
completely or the alveolar contact is deleted leaving
nasality in the preceding vowel phase, when the
following sound is /t/ ([ʔ]), e.g.

[wɑʔ] *want* (54)

[wʌõʔ] *won't* (61) x 2.

On the other hand, with /d/ following, /n/ is not
deleted, but the /d/ is, in accordance with the above
examples, e.g.

[fæɔn nɛm] *found them* (75).

In Shepherd's Bush and Peasmarsh, however, /t/ is
often deleted <u>after</u> /n/, when a vowel follows, e.g.

[dɪdn̩ ʌndəstæːmb] *didn't understand* Shepherd's Bush

[ka·n ɹivtʃ] *can't even* Peasmarsh (11).   (39)

Details of such differences from locality to locality
will be given in the separate chapters. (For a
detailed discussion of CCS in Stockport within a
dependency framework, see Lodge, 1981.)
    There is a special case of deletion of /d/, /v/
and /z/ in the auxiliary verb forms, such as *wouldn't,
haven't, doesn't* (cf. Petyt, 1978), which applies to
a large number of English accents, and is specific to
this class of verb. I do not intend to deal with
this in detail here, but clearly the conditions for
the deletion are not those of CCS.

(iv) *Unstressed vowel deletion (UVD)*
Another widespread feature of colloquial English is
the deletion of unstressed vowels, either completely
or by reduction to a glide. The commonest examples
of this, which applies to RP as well, are the so-
called weak forms of the auxiliary verbs, such as

10

I've, he's, we're. I shall not be concerned with
such forms in the individual localities, as they
occur in all of them. However, it is worth noting
that Zwicky (1972: 610-11) relates some of the
auxiliary contractions to a syntactic constraint,
distinguishing between "dependent" and "independent"
auxiliaries. The former, including *will, are* and *am,*
cannot contract unless they are in close syntactic
relation with the preceding word. Although this is
not the place to consider this in detail, in many
accents *will* is independent rather than dependent,
e.g.

> There's a man lives next door'll mend your
> fridge for you

is perfectly normal in Stockport. (See Lodge, 1979,
for a discussion of similar constructions in Stockport.) The contracted negative /nt/ is also discussed
by Zwicky (1972: 612-13) and he suggests that it
enters the phonological component in that form.
(Hasegawa, 1979: 136-37 suggests that such contractions should be handled in the lexicon.)
     The details of other types of UVD, which are
phonological processes, are locally varied and will
be given in each chapter. One of the commonest forms
of this process is the deletion of the first [ə] in
syllable sequences (regardless of word boundaries),
whose "full" rhythmic pattern is CV́CəCV̌, where C = at
least one consonant, as in *labourer* and *comfortable.*
E.g.

> [əpʌɔɫstʊə] *upholsterer* Stockport (37)

> [ɹɪmɛmbɹ əm] *remember them* Peasmarsh (35)

> [batɹe] *battery* Stockport (79).

The resultant cluster must be a possible English one
or the deletion cannot take place, e.g.

> *[hʌmblɪ ən] *humbler and.*

An example of the reduction to a glide is:

> [ðj ɐdmɪnɪstɹeʃn̩] *the administration* Edinburgh
> (29-30).

     A different environment in which an unstressed
vowel is sometimes deleted is where two consecutive
vowels come at a word-boundary: V # V.   In such
cases only one vowel remains, e.g.

> [ʃɛeʔʃe baœʔ] *shakes you about* Stockport (49).

11

(v) *Linking r and rhoticism*
The insertion of r between two vowels belonging to
different syllables is a widespread linking device
in English. The circumstances under which it is
used vary considerably from one area to another, and
even from one speaker to another. Even those speakers who use it widely do not always use it. The
following pairs of examples are by the same informant:

[fəʊ ɛedʒez] *for ages* Y, Stockport (57)

[ɛːdʊɛsə ɒp] *hairdresser up* Y, Stockport (56)

[endoəɹ ɛːɹeəl] *indoor aerial* N, Stockport (67)

[jə ɔːnnɹe] *your ordinary* N, Stockport (77)

[heə ən] *hair and* Shepherd's Bush (2)

[pʻɛɪpəɹ a] *paper I* Shepherd's Bush (3).

In accents with post-vocalic r the situation is somewhat different, since in a great many instances, e.g.
the six given above, the words end in /r/ anyway.
In such accents the variety of r used may be used as
a link between words where there is no final /r/,
e.g. *law of*, or the glottal stop may be used, e.g.

[ðə ʔæɑs] *the house* Peasmarsh (38).

(For words such as *comma* and *china* in rhotic accents,
see Wells, 1982: 221-22.)
       The status of /r/ is somewhat complicated in
English in that its incidence varies from one accent
to another. The difference between rhotic and non-
rhotic accents is in the occurrence or not of /r/
before a consonant. Thus, non-rhotic accents have no
alternating forms of words such as *farm, port, church*
and *perplex*, so such words have no underlying /r/, as
they do in rhotic accents. This reflects the inabil-
ity of non-rhotic speakers to predict correctly the
occurrence of word-internal, preconsonantal /r/.
(On this point, see Trudgill, 1980/83: esp. 148-49.)
On the other hand, word-final /r/, which is retained
before vowels even in non-rhotic accents, does
involve alternations, so that /r/ can be postulated
in the underlying forms of such words as *car, door,
fur* and *letter*. In the case of unstressed *-er* the
underlying form is syllabic: /r̩/, which may lose its
syllabicity by means of UVD. We need an /r/-deletion
rule to account for its non-occurrence before consonants, and the following realization rules for /r/:

12

$$/r/ \longrightarrow [\mathrm{\scriptstyle \theta}] / \underline{\quad\quad} \left\{ \begin{matrix} C \\ \emptyset \end{matrix} \right\}$$

$$\longrightarrow [\mathrm{\scriptstyle \theta_I}] / \underline{\quad\quad} \left\{ \begin{matrix} V \\ \underset{\mathrm{\scriptstyle I}}{r} \end{matrix} \right\}$$

$$/r/ \longrightarrow \emptyset / \underline{\quad\quad} \left\{ \begin{matrix} C \\ \emptyset \end{matrix} \right\}$$

Then there is /r/-insertion in those cases without underlying final /r/ for those people who have forms such as [lɔɹ əv] *law of* (for numerous examples, see Wells, 1982: 223-25). An alternative solution is not to postulate any underlying /r/ in word-final position either and simply have an /r/-insertion rule (cf. Wells, 1982: 222). However, the advantages of the former solution are (i) rhotic and non-rhotic accents have the same underlying forms in respect of final /r/, and (ii) it accounts for the fact that *soaring* has an /r/ but *sawing* does not for many speakers (cf. Wells, 1982: 225). Those who do have an r-sound in *sawing* etc. have extended the application of /r/-insertion, not differentiating between word-final and word-internal / ɔ /. There are even further extensions of /r/-insertion in some accents, e.g.

[jəɾ ɛniθiɡ̃] *you anything* Coventry (3)

[bəɪ̲ aːʔ] *by heart* Norwich (32).

(Cf. [tʼəɪ ëiʔ] *to eat*, Trudgill, 1974: 162; also Wells, 1982: 227. For some speakers in Norfolk even the indefinite article has linking /r/, e.g. [əɹæp̲ɫ] *a apple*.) Finally, we must note another type of speaker, who has no linking /r/ at all except word-internally, as in *nearest*, and uses [ʔ] instead. For them no underlying final /r/ is necessary.

To sum up, there are basically three types of speaker with regard to underlying /r/:
   (i)   Those with preconsonantal /r/ (rhotic);
   (ii) Those with word-final /r/ and /r/-deletion;
   (iii) Those without syllable-final /r/ and /r/-insertion.
/r/-insertion applies in different degrees for (i) and (ii), but for all three types the rule has the same phonetic formulation: any vowel lower than mid, i.e. [ə] and lower, whether long or short, stressed or unstressed, allows linking /r/ to follow before

another vowel. For speakers of type (iii), /ə/ not
/r/ appears in the underlying forms of *letter* etc.
There are also some speakers of type (ii) who delete
/r/ intervocalically, as in [veɪ] *very*, giving the
same output as (iii) for words ending in /r/ before
a vowel. The following derivations give alternative
pronunciations of *quarter of* for (ii) and (iii).

(ii)   /kwɔtr̩ ɒv/

        Stress placement ⇒ kwɔ́tr̩ əv

        /r/-realization   ⇒ kwɔ́tər əv

UVD ⇒ [kwɔ́tr̩ əv]   /r/-deletion ⇒ kwɔ́tə əv

                         UVD   ⇒ [kwɔ́təv]

(iii)   /kwɔ́tə ɒv/

        Stress placement ⇒ kwɔ́tə əv

UVD ⇒ [kwɔ́təv]   [ʔ]-insertion ⇒ [kwɔ́tə ʔəv]

(The /t/ can also be realized as [ʔ].)

PANLECTAL AND POLYLECTAL GRAMMARS
One problem to which this book is intended as a
contribution is how far one system underlies all
varieties of a language. This assumption (often
implicit) may seem attractive at first sight in that
it accounts for the notion of <u>one language</u>: all
speakers of the same language have the same basic
system with the variants accounted for by fairly late,
realization rules, rule order differences and the
like. It seems reasonable to suppose that if speakers
of the same language can understand each other, then
they must have the same basic system underlying their
performance. However, mutual intelligibility is not
a simple yes/no question. There are different degrees
of intelligibility, there is intelligibility in one
way only, and furthermore mutual intelligibility cuts
across generally accepted language boundaries. For
example, broad dialect speakers from Devon and Durham
will have considerable difficulty understanding one
another, whereas similarly broad speakers from Leeds
and Liverpool will have far fewer problems of communication, though there may well be some. Secondly, we
must note that none of these speakers have any difficulty in understanding RP as used on the radio and
television, whereas speakers of RP often have difficulty in understanding broad regional accents.
Thirdly, with regard to the artificiality of language

boundaries, a Low German speaker living near the Dutch-German border has more in common linguistically with his near Dutch neighbours than with his Bavarian compatriots. Fourthly, it sometimes happens that two speakers can understand each other using different languages (cf. Dorian's study of Gaelic and English in East Sutherland, 1982), indicating that mutual intelligibility is certainly not a sufficient criterion. Chomsky (1980: 117-20) concludes that the notion of language is of little use to linguists, who, in his view, should concentrate on grammars not languages.
  We must also take account of the speaker's knowledge of his/her own system. Our example of one-way intelligibility demonstrates that it is possible for a speaker of one variety to understand another without necessarily being able to reproduce it. Let us give a more specific example to clarify the point. Northern English (i.e. not Scottish) speakers do not differentiate between [ʊ] and [ʌ] in their own systems, whereas Southern speakers, and RP speakers, do, as in *put* and *putt* respectively. Nevertheless, Northerners can understand radio and television news bulletins spoken with an RP accent, and Southerners can understand not-too-broad Northerners with respect to this distinction. But, if we observe Northerners and Southerners trying to mimic their counterparts (for whatever reason), we soon see that there are two separate vowel systems. A number of Northern speakers (who were not brought up to do so) try to use the [ʊ]/[ʌ] distinction: they use an unrounded vowel, somewhere in the region of [æ̈] or [ə̣], for both sounds. (See below for further discussion of this from a social point of view.) Thus we hear not only [kæm] *come* and [sæ̈n] *son, sun*, but also [pæt] *put* and [bætʃə] *butcher*. These speakers simply do not know, in the technical, linguistic sense, the difference between these two sounds. Similarly, Southern-born actors portraying Northerners often forget to use [ʊ] for both sounds, using the occasional [ʌ] in accordance with their own system: they, for their part, do not know the lack of difference.
  Misunderstandings between speakers of different regional varieties of a language are a useful source of evidence for linguists; many examples of this kind of occurrence are very enlightening from the point of view of underlying systems. If we are attempting to establish a theory of language which claims to explain how native speakers understand each other, we must also investigate how it is they often misunderstand each other as well, because even in perfect conditions

15

of communication misunderstandings occur. For
instance, in a seminar about the language of comedy
shows I mentioned the expression [t'ɹɒbɫ ə? ?mɪɫ]
(*trouble at the mill*). A student from the London
area wrote this down subsequently in an essay as
trouble up mill. In terms of her phonological system
[ə?] followed by a bilabial closure could only be
interpreted as *up*. Furthermore, because she was un-
used to the use of a glottal stop for the definite
article, she was unable to detect the longer hold
period of the glottal stop (during which the lips are
brought together) in comparison with the hold period
where no definite article occurs, as in *trouble at
Manchester*. In a detailed transcription of the two
utterances this difference can be indicated as
follows:

    [ə? p̚m] as in *at the mill*,

    [ə?m] as in *at Manchester*.

(It should be pointed out that the use of two joined
letter symbols in the first transcription gives in
this visual form an impression of greater length
than is, in fact, involved, but this is one of the
problems of letter transcriptions.)
    Trudgill (1983a) presents the results of two
tests designed to ascertain the degree of predicta-
bility of syntactic forms and semantic interpretations
from various English dialects. These show that, for
the most part, linguistically sophisticated native
speakers, even those with considerable training and
experience in linguistics, fare little better than
foreigners in predicting possible sentences of some
varieties of English. On the basis of this kind of
evidence it is difficult to see how a panlectal
grammar is justifiable, and whether even a polylectal
approach is appropriate.
    It is worth noting how children deal with variant
forms. If there are variant forms within the child's
immediate circle of adult models, it will tend to
waver in its usage and this may well persist in adult
speech; for instance, P's use of both [boˑk] and
[bok] for *book*, Lodge, 1983, and Y's use of both
[lɪɒk] and [lok] for *look* in Chapter 1 below, because
both had in their immediate family speakers who used
the diphthongal variant and also those who used the
monophthongal variant in such words. If a child is
exposed to regional variants only sporadically, up to
about the age of 3 or 4, it often handles them phonetically, that is to say, it imitates them; thus, a
child of Southern parents, exposed to a Northern

neighbour's [a] in *bath*, will sometimes mimic the [a]-pronunciation. When it is older, however, the child will tend to handle the Northern pronunciations phonologically, that is, it will reinterpret them in terms of its own system and will no longer attempt to mimic them. (This is based on personal observation during 12 years' residence in Norfolk, and it needs much more careful and rigorous investigation.) At some stage during the acquisition process a child learns the equivalences between those alien accents to which it is exposed and its own system. This would suggest that all speakers, whatever their phonological system, learn a set of equivalences for the English "language", but only those to which they are exposed. If we follow Trudgill (1983a: 29-30), we need to separate the native speaker competence from the speaker's ability to understand varieties other than his/her own. In other words competence is restricted to the native speaker's knowledge of the forms he/she produces normally. Of course, many such grammars overlap and this explains a speaker's ability to understand other, not-too-dissimilar varieties. Where varieties differ, a speaker will use a number of different techniques, both linguistic and pragmatic, to attempt a suitable interpretation of what he/she has heard. If a speaker is in regular contact with a different variety, then one technique of comprehension would be a set of equivalence rules. These are not performance rules, but recognition techniques. They would be of the sort Trudgill discusses (1974: 140-44) for relating the different subsystems in Norwich, e.g.

$$// \bar{a} // \atop // ai //\;\Big\} \to \; // ai //.$$

This is the rule used by many Norwich speakers for collapsing the phonological difference between lexical items such as *name* and *nail* (see further Chapter 6, below). In the case of RP/Stockport, there would be a rule collapsing the *put/putt* distinction:

$$/ ʌ / \atop / u /\;\Big\} \to \; / o /\;(^5).$$

As an example of a rule relating Stockport and RP, we can give the following:

$$/\varepsilon\mathrm{I}/\ \Big\}\ \rightarrow\ /\mathrm{ej}/$$
$$/\mathrm{e:}/$$

which collapses the distinction found in older Stockport speakers between *weight* with a diphthong and
wait with a long monophthong. We must stress that
equivalence rules are learnt optionally, if the
(social) need for them arises, e.g. a move to a new
part of the country. A second aspect of variety comprehension that
needs further investigation is the quantification of
the degree of difference between dialects (cf.
Trudgill, 1983a: 30). We need to establish a method
of predicting mutual intelligibility, or otherwise,
of different accents. Both phonological distinctions
and phonetic realization are relevant to this. In a
test similar to that discussed by Trudgill (1983a),
already mentioned above, which I administered to a
number of language and linguistics undergraduates
from various parts of the United Kingdom at the
University of East Anglia ([6]), the pronunciation
[bʌ˩] for *bull* was rejected by Southerners and RP-
speakers as non-English, no doubt on the phonological
grounds of lexical incidence, but by many speakers
from the North of England it was perceived as "posh"
or even "RP", presumably a misinterpretation of the
RP vowel system on the basis of phonetic confusion
(see also above in this section). Similarly, [stɹɛː]
for *straw* is likely to cause considerable difficulty
of comprehension for any speaker who says [stɹɔː] for
this word because of the phonetic distance of the two
vowel phases and also because of the phonetic simi-
larity of the former to the more common pronunciations
of *stray*.
          As a starting-point, then, I shall not assume
the same basic underlying pan-English system for all
the varieties I shall investigate. The present book
is intended as a contribution to determine what all
English accents do have in common and what distin-
guishes them one from another. There is sufficient
evidence to conclude that, rather than assume an
idealized speaker/hearer who has a system which is
represented by formal standard spoken English, it is
important to use colloquial data on which to test
hypotheses (cf. Lodge, 1976 and 1979; J. Milroy, 1982:
46-47). I shall not attempt to give an exhaustive
account of the phonological system of each locality;
rather I have selected those distinctions and processes that are necessary for the comparison of areal
and social differences.

HISTORICAL BACKGROUND
Another aspect of variety which has to be considered
in attempting to establish a speaker's competence of
his/her community is the historical background to the
differentiation of local varieties, and the extent to
which this can legitimately be said to form part of
that competence. An extreme example of use of historical background in establishing a phonological
system is furnished by Chomsky and Halle (1968),
where details of the Great Vowel Shift are assumed
to underlie the modern English vowel system, and, to
quote a particular example, an underlying velar
fricative is posited to account for the difference
in the stressed vowels in *righteous* and *divinity*
(ibid.: 234). If we consider change on a smaller
scale, we find instances of competing and obsolescent
forms, which have to be considered when establishing
the phonological systems of a community. A few
examples will suffice to demonstrate this aspect of
accent varieties. Around Manchester there are three
forms of the word *father* in respect of the stressed
vowel: [fáðə], [féeðə] (or an alternative with a
monophthong, [fé:ðə], depending on the quality of
the vowel in words such as *gate* and *name*), and
[fé:ðə], the first two being considered old-fashioned
by most speakers in the Stockport area. The first
one, with its short vowel, is the modern reflex of
the oblique forms in Middle English, e.g. genitive
fadres, which has been regularized to the subject
form as well. The second pronunciation is from the
Middle English nominative, *fader*. In this case the
short *a* was lengthened at a later period because it
was in an open syllable, that is, *fa-der*; this then
changed its quality, monophthongal or diphthongal,
along with other words of this type, e.g. *name*, *gate*.
The third pronunciation is a borrowing from the
standard pronunciation, perhaps via the church. Although all three forms are known to Stockport speakers,
as obsolescent forms, the first two would normally
only be used facetiously (cf. Lodge, 1973: 86, footnote). On the other hand, in parts of Lancashire
their status is different, all three being current in
different groups of the community: the first two are
used by many speakers over 50 years old and some
younger ones in rural areas, the exact distribution
of each being unknown to me, and the borrowed form is,
in general, used by those under the age of 50. Sporadic use of the older forms by younger speakers would
seem to be an indication of regional awareness, as
opposed to facetiousness in the case of Stockport.
Interpretation of any form by local speakers will

help to determine its status in the system. In the case of the first two forms in Stockport, they are like fossils, learnt piecemeal, and can be represented as a listing in the grammar (even though they are the historically more "correct" forms). The same would apply to similar forms such as [kɔɪl] for *coal* (possibly a loan-pronunciation from Yorkshire rather than a relic), and [ɹɪiʔ] and [nɪiʔ] for *right* and *night* (cf. Lodge, 1973: 86), which are reflexes of the retention of the velar fricative referred to above in such words longer in the North of England than in the South, so that development along with words of the *fine*-type did not take place. (The /ɔɞ/-diphthong referred to in Lodge, 1973: 84, is even more of a rarity in Stockport; I have only ever heard it used regularly by one speaker, Y's father (see Chapter 1), in one word only: *Shaw* [ʃɔɞ] *Heath*, a district of Stockport.)

To make decisions on historical matters of this sort with regard to establishing the present system of a locality, we must have regard to whether such alternatives are known (in the technical sense) as regular forms, facetious forms, "odd" forms, and so on. We can even see cases of change in progress. For example, the /ɛɪ/-/eː/ distinction mentioned above (p.18) and discussed in Lodge (1973) is not known by a large number of speakers in the Stockport area, namely those who have a diphthong in *name*, *gate* and *wait* anyway, and this can apply to members of the same family: thus, of the six members of Y's and N's family (see Chapter 1; Lodge, 1966, 1978 and 1983), three, including N, used the distinction, three, including Y, did not. A similar case is furnished by Norwich speakers: older members of certain groups have a distinction between the vowels of *gate* with /ɛː/ and *day* with /æɪ/, whereas the majority of young speakers do not have the distinction and do not know how to apply it. (This calls into question the exact interpretation of diasystem by Trudgill, 1974: 134-5, as a system common to all members of the speech community. Cf. also his own comments on this in Trudgill, 1983a: 11-12.)

LANGUAGE AND SOCIAL GROUPS
As a final consideration I now want to look at some of the social aspects of phonological variation. Since variant forms can occur within one locality and even in one and the same speaker's utterances, it is generally assumed that this variation has some kind of social significance of a group-membership kind, whereby a speaker indicates which group of people he/

she wishes to be associated with. This kind of variation is obviously different from the stylistic variation which is determined by application or otherwise of allegro rules, etc., though there may be some overlap. For example, the incidence of [?] in Stockport can be used as an indication of group membership (see further on this below), whereas the deletion of unstressed vowels is a feature of fast speech in all speakers in Stockport. On the other hand, the fast-speech feature of place of articulation harmony may be applied differentially by different groups, for example, teenagers use it more than speakers who are over sixty years old ([7]).

Much research in this area has concentrated on relating sets of linguistic variants to given social groups (e.g. Labov, 1980; Trudgill, 1974; Trudgill and Foxcroft, 1978). These groups are intuitive/ traditional or based on some official set of categories (those of the Registrar General in Britain). However, it is becoming more and more evident that these categories are too gross to be of much practical value to the linguist and much finer distinctions are made by some researchers (e.g. Milroy and Milroy, 1978; Milroy, 1980; Cheshire, 1982). In what has come to be called correlational linguistics, sophisticated statistical techniques are employed to present the data in quantified terms([8]), relating patterns of variation sometimes to predetermined socio-economic groups, sometimes to smaller social groups.

As far as British English is concerned, it is the smaller social unit which seems to be the most fruitful area of research (cf. Milroy's comments, 1980: 13-14). Variety in many British contexts groups people together in a way which cuts across any socio-economic groups. It may well be that in other English-speaking countries the grosser class unit is sufficient to cope with discernible variation (though note McEntegart and Le Page's caveat about assuming knowledge of stratification of a foreign community, 1982: 123), but in the area where I have most experience, Stockport, terms like "middle class" and "working class" are very difficult to apply. It is important to stress that from the point of view of evaluation by other speakers, we have to deal with relative classifications. For example, many Southern British speakers classify Northerners as working class, even if their accent has only a few regional features. On the other hand, within the Stockport area there are many subtle differences, which only local speakers are aware of. For instance, to many speakers in Stockport the pronunciation [a:f] for *half*, rather than [af],

in times of the clock, e.g. *half past three*, would
be considered "snobbish, posh". This is a question
of social status rather than of social class.
What I would like to propose is that there are
a number of social groups within a geographical area,
which are determined by a number of linguistic features. In other words, linguistic variation is not
seen as a reflection of some *a priori* system of
social classification, but rather as one of the
factors which go towards dividing people up into
social groups. (Cf. Cheshire's, 1982, discussion of
non-standard features of Reading English.) I can
exemplify this by using the distribution of the
glottal stop in Stockport (⁹). This shows the
following characteristics:

A: occurrence in word-final position as a
   variant of [t] or [k], and in glottally
   reinforced variants of [p̃], [t̃] and [k̃];

B: glottally reinforced variants of [p̃], [t̃]
   and [k̃], and as a variant of [t] in
   syllable-final position before consonants;

C: as A, plus occurrence in intervocalic
   position within a word, and use as the
   definite article;

D: as B, plus occurrence as the definite
   article.

These regularly occurring groups of linguistic variants equate in general with the following groups of
people:

A = teenage girls;

B = women of 50 and older;

C = teenage boys;

D = men of 50 and older.

Some speakers show considerable variation in use,
others are more consistent. Association with different groups in different contexts on the level of
interpersonal encounters can be explained in terms
of accommodation (see, for example, Giles and
Powesland, 1975: esp. 154-81). When two speakers
shift their accents slightly, each in the direction
of the other, their accents converge; when two speakers emphasize the differences between their accents,
they diverge. (For a discussion of the social
reasons for this, see Giles and Powesland, ibid.)
In the Stockport example, speakers will choose
particular forms depending on which group they want

to be identified with. In certain cases the forms
chosen by a speaker will produce an evaluation by
other speakers. For example, at home a teenage girl
may conform to type A, but out with her peers in the
evening, she may well use forms of type C. Members
of other groups, for example her parents, will tend
to react adversely to certain forms not associated
with her "normal" group, e.g. the use of the glottal
stop as the definite article, and classify her as
"common" or a "tomboy".

In the same way we can interpret the use of
forms such as [kæm] *come* and [bætʃə] *butcher*,
mentioned above, as an attempt on the part of the
speaker to associate with a group considered by them
to be worthy of emulation - RP-speakers. On the other
hand, other groups, for example, members of a Stockport working-men's club, will not be impressed by such
pronunciations and will interpret them as low-valued.
As a mark of their solidarity in contrast to the
aspirations implicit in the RP-emulation, they will
use the local forms with /o/, which they value more
highly, and on occasion use "broader" forms such as
[nɪi?] rather than [näː?] for *night* (cf. Lodge, 1973:
86). In addition to this we may note that as people
change their social role, they operate with different
systems of evaluation depending on the circumstances;
thus a speaker who regularly emulates RP may also use
indigenous /o/-forms ([10]) regularly, when talking to
close relatives of their own sex, as a mark of solidarity.

We are, therefore, concerned with classification
into social groups by fellow-members of a community
via the linguistic forms used, as well as by the
linguist-observer. The members of a community are on
the whole not conscious of the linguistic indices that
they use to classify other speakers (though there is,
of course, a certain amount of *ad hoc* conscious
knowledge of linguistic differences); it is the
linguist's task to identify them. Although much work
has been done on individual indices, more investigation of the interrelationships of sets of indices
is necessary, if we are to progress beyond a piecemeal appreciation of their role.

Although in this book I shall not be going into
detail with regard to the indices of the various
social groupings within each locality, leaving that
for the future, I am assuming that the phonological
differences that I discuss in each chapter form at
least part of the total set of indices differentiating
British English accents, that is, some of the ways
whereby an Englishman can recognize a Scotsman, some-

one from Oldham can recognize someone from Stockport, and a chartered accountant can recognize a road-mender.

NOTES

[1]. In a very simple test I asked a number of unsophisticated English speakers to make a noun from *opaque*, by asking them to fill in the missing word in the second of the two following sentences, keeping the meaning the same: *Look at that glass - it's opaque. Look at the ...... of that glass.* In most cases there was no immediate response, but when a word was offered, it was invariably *opaqueness*, avoiding the Latinate alternation altogether. For a more thorough test and discussion, see Cutler (1980).

[2]. It is quite likely that alternations of the *school - scholar, join - junction* type, as discussed by Ladefoged (1982: 82) should be treated in terms of relational rules (cf. Tiersma, 1983: 73-76) rather than process rules, as a reflection of their fossilized nature.

[3]. /ʌ/ is an exception (see below), but this has nothing to do with morphological alternations.

[4]. The matching of the voice feature in the preceding context of CCS obviates the necessity of proposing a dependency degree of 3 for the deleted stops (cf. Lodge, 1981). The environments are treated differently by Guy (1980) and Neu (1980) and the rule is treated polylectally. The hierarchy of constraining environments is difficult to test on the material presented here, but I would not consider it valid for British English. Guy's notion of articulatory complexity of the cluster (1980: 9) deserves further investigation, but his morphological conditioning, referred to *passim*, does not seem to hold in the data recorded from my informants.

[5]. In Trudgill's example he uses the double slant lines to indicate units of the diasystemic phonological inventory. I am not concerned here with the notion of diasystem, so I simply use single slants.

[6]. For details, see Lodge (in preparation).

[7]. For a statistical treatment of one such phonological feature, t/d-deletion, see Guy (1980).

[8]. A full list of such works would be very large, but see, for example, Sankoff (1978), Trudgill (1978), Labov (1980), Romaine (1982), and the references therein. For a critique of such methods, see McEntegart and Le Page (1982).

[9]. For further details of Stockport speech, see Lodge (1966; female, aged 68), Lodge (1973) and (1978;

24

female, aged 16), as well as Chapter 1 of the present
book. In addition I have drawn on my personal obser-
vations over many years.
  [10]. We must note that although the terms *hyper-
correction* and *hyperdialectalism* are used to describe
certain forms (e.g. Trudgill, 1983a: 12), there is no
justification for establishing "true" dialects from
which certain accents deviate. (Cf. Petyt's comments
on this, 1980: 27-28.) Thus, the accent with [æ̈]
rather than [ɒ] is merely a realizational variant
belonging to those accents without the [ʌ]/[ɒ] distinction.

GENERAL CONVENTIONS

The format of each chapter (except the final one)
follows the same pattern. First, a general description of the phonetic features of the informant(s)
including vowel diagrams, followed by the transcription of the recording of the informant(s). The
extracts have been chosen to exemplify all the
characteristic features of the speaker's accent
occurring in the recording. Finally, each phonological process displayed by the informant(s) is
discussed in detail.

The transcription follows the conventions of the
IPA with the following exceptions: (i) stress is
marked with an acute accent over the vowel of the
syllable in question (in order to avoid making
decisions about syllable boundaries); (ii) labiodental stops are written [π] and [ψ] for voiceless
and voiced respectively; (iii) glottally reinforced
sounds are written with the glottal stop symbol
immediately above the other symbol: [ʔt], [ʔk]; (iv)
the retroflex approximant is represented by [ɹ];
(v) affrication is marked with a following ['ʃ]; (vi)
creaky voice is shown by a subscript tilde: [a̰]; if
there is no symbol above the tilde this indicates an
indistinct vocoid transition. The following points
should also be noted: I have marked unreleased stops
with [˺] before other oral stops and before a pause;
otherwise they are released slightly or into the
following sounds; I have not always marked aspiration
of the voiceless stops: these are sometimes described
in the general remarks of the locality and only particularly noticeable aspiration is marked in the transcription; where [ʔ] is written between two homorganic
stops (nasal or oral), the supraglottal closure is
assumed to continue throughout the sequence, thus
[nʔn] is written rather than [nʔ̃n]. It is assumed
that all unstressed vowels are centralized in comp-

26

arison with their stressed counterparts. Partially
nasalized long vowel phases have the tilde over the
second part of the symbolization only, eg. [ʌɔ̃],
[aɪ̃].
     The layout of the transcription indicates breath
groups: | in the phonetic transcription, / in the
orthography, and a new block (separated from the
previous one by its orthographic version) indicates
that another speaker has been speaking or that a
considerable extract has been omitted. Hesitations
and trailing off are indicated by dots. The orthographic version is not punctuated in any standard
way; it is only a guide to the transcription. In
citations in the text I have omitted irrelevant
diacritics, in particular, stress marks.
     Since I am not concerned in this book with the
exact phonological interpretation of the vowel
systems of the different localities, I shall simply
use the most common phonetic form to represent them,
as appropriate (see especially Chapter 7). In each
locality I have given vowel diagrams for the most
commonly occurring articulations of each informant.
Where there are no instances of a known vowel, this
has been noted. The dots indicating the positions
of the vowels on the diagrams are a typographical
convenience and represent an idealization of the
variation within the vowel space. For RP vowels in
examples I have used a simplified broad transcription.
     I have used two abbreviations for book titles
throughout:
     SED = Orton, H. et al. <u>Survey of English</u>
<u>Dialects, Volumes I - IV</u>.
     SPE = Chomsky, A. N. and Halle, M. <u>The Sound</u>
<u>Pattern of English</u>.

Map showing the localities

E = Edinburgh   S = Stockport
C = Coventry   N = Norwich
SB = Shepherd's Bush   P = Peasmarsh

Chapter One

STOCKPORT, GREATER MANCHESTER
(until 1974, in Cheshire)

The two informants from Stockport represent two
different generations of the same family. Speaker Y
is 16 years old and attends a comprehensive school
in Stockport. She is the grand-daughter of speaker
N, who is 77 years old. Although the grandfather
lived in China for two years as a very small child,
he has lived and worked in Stockport for the rest of
his life. Speaker Y has lived all her life in Stockport too; although most of her friends are likewise
local teenagers, she has several friends in Liverpool.
(Speaker N's wife is the informant for Lodge, 1966.)

(i) *General*
(For a detailed description of the phonetic characteristics of speaker Y see Lodge, 1978: 56-61.)
Closures in the oral cavity tend to be more weakly
articulated by Y than by N. This means that stops
and fricatives can be found in different utterances
of the same word, e.g. [pɛpəz] and [pɛɸəz] for
Pepper's. It also means that many of the stop
releases are slow giving an affricated sound, e.g.
[lɛtˢə] and [lɛtsə] for *letter*. Note that this
explains the creaky voice following occurrences of
the glottal stop, e.g. [gɑʔə̰] *got a*. Speaker N, on
the other hand, does not have this feature. The
normal lip position for both speakers is neutral.
Such rounding as does occur is effected by parting
the lips in the centre only so that the sides are
kept together. The one exception is [ø:], where the
lips protrude slightly. There is in speaker Y a
predisposition to use labio-dental articulations.
This is particularly noticeable with her r-sound:[ʋ].
A labio-dental closure is also often used as the
position of rest, e.g. [doɱ] *done* at the end of a
whole utterance. It must be stressed that this tendency to use labio-dental articulations is not caused

by a protrusion of the top teeth or some similar
physical characteristic. It is a widespread feature
of speakers from various parts of Lancashire and
Cheshire, particularly common amongst teenagers and
younger children.

(ii) *Vowel diagrams*

Speaker Y:

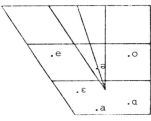

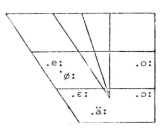

short monophthongs   long monophthongs

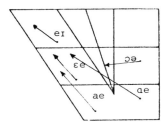

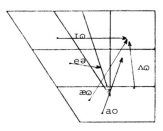

front closing   back closing
diphthongs   diphthongs
and [ɔə]   and [eə]

Speaker N:

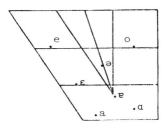

short monophthongs

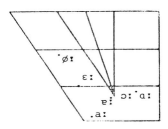

long monophthongs

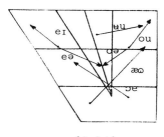

diphthongs

(There are no examples of [εe] in the extract.)

Neutral lip positions are indicated by using the IPA
symbol for unrounded vowels; [e: ɛ: a:] are produced
with lips spread rather than neutral by speaker Y.
Note that [ɐ:] and [a:] are produced with the same
tongue height and retraction but are differentiated by
the lip position, neutral versus spread respectively.

(iii) *The transcription of speaker Y*

1   ɐ gáʔ guéeψ uán en éŋgleʃ léʔ so m tʼɛ́eken ɛ́e lɛvɫ̩ néçʃ ɟéə

I got grade one in English Lit., so I'm taking A-level next
year.

2   sɛɸ̃ ʔáʔ wan

Except that one.

3   aé ɛ́etʼ eʔ

I hate it.

4   ɐ̥ uéəɫe uáz gʌ̊ɶeŋ tʼ ˡꞬ

I   really was going to ...

5   ɐ wɛ́ŋʔ fəu éntʼəvjíɶz boʔ ðe séz ɐ wɒŋʔ gód enof | so ɐ
6   θaˑʔ uáeʔ je kʼən stéʔ je dʒáβ ðɛ̃

I went for interviews but they says I wasn't good enough /
so I thought right, you can stick your job then.

7   ɐ wɛ́ŋʔ fə | kədɛ́ʔ kɑ́ːs kas ɐ wʊ́nʔ ʌ̊ɫd enof tʼə gʌ̊ɶ tʼə
8   nɵ̃ːsen | boʔ ʃe séz ɐ ɛŋʔ gáʔ enof ʌ̊ɶ lɛvɫ̩z ɐ wʊ́nʔ díɶen
9   enof so ʃe woɫ̩ʔ geβ me nˑ ɐplekʼɛ́eʃɫ̩ fám

I went for / cadet course 'cos I wasn't old enough to go to
nursing / but she says I ain't got enough O-levels I wasn't
doing enough so she wouldn't give me an application form.

10 ɐ gáʔ ə dʒáb en ə sí̃ɶpmmmɛ́ːkeʔ ɛ̃ staʔpɔəʔ ʔs dʒost ʌ̊ɶpmd̥ |
11 je ɛndʒáe jesɛ́ɫ

I got a job in a supermarket in Stockport that's just
opened / You enjoy yourself.

12 no naʔ áːɫ lə tʼáːm ðɛ tʼɛek eʔ en tʼɵ̃̃ːz laeʔ je nʌ̊ɶ tʼə
13 ueléɪ̥v péɪɸo wɛn nɛe gʌ̊ɶ fˑ ðɛː buéek̥ ɫ̩ stóf laeʔ ða̰ʔ | eʔs

32

14 ɑ: ʋáeʔ je áv ə láf we ðəm á: jə no·

No, not all the time they take it in turns like you know
to relieve people when they go for their break and stuff
like that. / It's all right, you have a laugh with them
all you know.

15 θɹéɪ pɛ́:z en ðə bén | ð dósbemmɛ́n ɐd ə pɛ́:ɹ éɪtʃ ən éɪ

16 néʔt ə pɛ́:

Three pairs in the bin / The dustbinmen had a pair each
and he nicked a pair.

17 á·ᵽ doṹʔ ʋɛ́kʧ so·

I don't reckon so.

18 ef ðe sɛ́e jɐv t'ɛ́m meneʔ t'eɪ bʋɛ́ek ɐv ɛ́:f ən áoə
         °
If they say you have a ten-minute tea break, I have half
an hour.

19 ʎ̃ɔvət'á:m ən stóf laeʔ ʔáʔ so ɐ góvə n̩ ə sónde sómt'á:mz
                           ̃   °
Overtime and stuff like that, so I go over on a Sunday
sometimes.

20 ðe gɛ́ʔ sɛ́vnt'e fáeβ pɛ́ns ən ǽɔə | sɛ́vʧ páoŋψ fɛ́fte
          '
They get 75 pence an hour / seven pound fifty.

21 ðe dóɪ̃ʔ stɛe ʎ̃ɔpn̩ ðe dʒos sták oɸ ʃɛ́ɫvz
                     '   ° °
They don't stay open they just stock up shelves.

22 ɐ gáʔ t'ʎ̃ɔɫd af t'ʎ̃ɔɫd ɐg gɛ́ʔ ðə sák kɑs ɐg gáʔ ʔtɛ́ɫ dʒámd

I got told off told I'd get the sack 'cos I'd got the till
jammed.

23 eʔs dʒós ʋaeʔ ápəzepˀ bʋéteʃ ʎ̃ɔm stɔ́əz

It's just right opposite British Home Stores.

24 jɛ́: eʔs zə kɫáseks nǽɔ ᵏgatˀ t'íɔ bég sénəməz zɛ́: | eʔs

25 ɫá:k je ʋá:ʔ op ðɛ́: ə̃j jə líɔkeʊ ʋá:ʔ dǽɔn ɐt' eʔ

Yeah it's the Classics now, it's got two big cinemas there.
/ It's like you're right up there and you're looking right
down at it.

33

26 e? kaʃ°ᵉ tʃwɛ́n:ᵈe faːβ pɛ́ns aŋ n̥ə βós

It costs you twenty-five pence on the bus.

27 féfteɪm pɛ́ns | tévəψö ént e? | ?e?s ó:fɫ áː gɛ? əwɛ we fó:
28 ðʌω | puesɛ́nd aŋ óndə se?stéɪn | sʌω ɐkt̮ gɛ́? əwɛ́e weð e?
29 je nə | je gɛ́? soŋ ʊáe? déːt'e ɫó?s af ðə kəndóktəz zʌω |
30 ðɛɾ áːɫ | dɛ́d jóŋ

Fifteen pence / Terrible, isn't it? / It's awful I get away
with four though / Pretend I'm under sixteen / so I can get
away with it you know / You get some right dirty looks off
the conductors though. / They're all / dead young.

31 ?tʃéendʒ ũɐ̯ maˑenḓ | máend³ jíω we máe ɛː ðɛd̮ tʃó? me ǽω? |
32 ef je gɛ́? je ɛ́ː ko? lae? ðá? β̃ ná? komen éə

I changed my mind / Mind you with my hair they'd chuck me
out / If you get your hair cut like that I'm not coming
here.

33 ɐ lóv aven ə móg ə tʃéken síωp̄ befáʊ ɐ ɣó t'ə bɛd wɛn ɐw̃
34 wátʃeṇ n̥ə t'ɛ́le

I love having a mug of chicken soup before I go to bed when
I'm watching the telly.

35 ez ə wóḡ ko? məʃéɪnestˤ | wǿ:?çs op áfət'ən | e ast'ə k'ó?
36 áːɫ pɛ́ɪsez ə wód je nʌω ɾaek' ə̃ mɛ́ek θéŋz

He's a wood-cut machinist / works up Offerton / He has to
cut all pieces of wood you know like and make things.

37 e ɛ́e?s e? e láˑe??ᵗ ðə wán e ád͡b̄ befáːʊ e wz n əpʌωɫstʊə

He hates it, he liked the one he had before, he was an
upholsterer.

38 e sɛ́ḓ ðə fɛ́ɫə ðɛ́ː t'ʌωɫm me t'ə gʌω daonstéːz weɣ som stˤóɸ
39 wɛ́e?t̮ fə | t'ə be dón e sɛz ɐ θáːt' e? b̄ be sóm sɛt'ˤéɪz
40 waŋπ ʊeɪk'óvʊen ə sómθen

He said the fellow there told me to go downstairs we've
some stuff waiting for / to be done he says I thought it'd
be some settees want recovering or something.

41 job̄ bɛ́?ə léɪv ðáˑ? t̮ gɛ? nóðə wán

34

You'd better leave that and get another one.

42 me mɛ́eʔ wɛ́nde ʃɛ́ɪj beŋ góen ǽœʔ weð ə láð fə ... | á·β beŋ

43 góen ǽœʔ we ẽw t'íꭥ ŋ ɛ́:f jéəz ɑn sǽt'əde so we ɑ́ wentʼ t'ə

44 blá?pɪꭥɫ se sɛ́ɫəbɾɛeʔ | wɑ̃ɪ̃ led wəz sék'ɑ́n eʔ ə̃ fel tə́ũψ

45 ʊáoṇd tə ez gíʏ fʊénd e sɛz ez e ɑ́:ʊ ʊá:ʔ

My mate Wendy she's been going out with a lad for ... /
I've been going out with him two and a half years on Saturday, so we all went to Blackpool to celebrate. / One lad
was sick on it and Phil turned round to his girl-friend he
says, Is he all right?

46 ɑ́: lóvd eʔ | ðə bégꜟ dépə waw̃ʔ wǿ:k'en no

I loved it / The Big Dipper wasn't working, though.

47 ɐ θɑ́·ʔ weᵊz góen t'ə go ɑ́f əʔ ðə k'ɑ́:nə kəz eʔ dʒǿ:ʔt' ən

48 eʔ sɛ́ɪm t'ə t'ép óp

I thought we was going to go off at the corner 'cos it
jerked and it seemed to tip up.

49 we wɛ́ə̃ʔ aṇ ṇaʔ n̰ eʔ ʊát'ɫz ɑ: ɫə t'ɑ́:m | ʃɛ́eʔʃe bǽœʔ

We went on that and it rattles all the time / shakes you
about.

50 ðɛ mɛ́eʔ je

They make you.

51 ʃe mɑ́:ʔ ə gat' én jɛʔ | ʔ depɛ́nnz ef ʃez pɑ́st əʊ éŋɫəʃ |

52 ef ʃe dóʒ̥ ʃe be ɛ́ebə t'ə béɪ | ə | nǿ:s

She might have got in yet / It depends if she's passed her
English. / If she does, she'll be able to be / a / nurse.

53 sómθeɪ̃ laeʔ ðɑ́ʔ | ʃe domꜟ bɑ́ðə

Something like that / She doesn't bother.

54 ɐ waʔ ə dɑ́·g̊ | ðjos t'ɐv lᴧ̃ꭥdz

I want a dog / They used to have loads.

55 ɐ k'ó? ðes pɛ́?tʃʊ ǽəʔ ʔə pɛ́epə ṇ ṇés gíəɫ ʃe̥ ad lóvle hɛ́: |

56 t'óx eʔ t'ə ðe ɛ́:dʊɛsə op ðə ʊᴧ̃ꭥd

35

I cut this picture out of the paper and this girl she had
lovely hair / Took it to the hairdresser up the road.

57 ɐ k'έπ ᵐe έʮ̃ kɔ́vəd ɔ́π fəʊ έedʒez | laɐk ə nɔ́ʔt'ə

I kept my head covered up for ages / Like a nutter.

58 jɪɷ ɬok á:fɬ so ɐ k'ɔ́t' eʔ t'ə mέek eʔ lɪ́ɷʔ bέt'ə k'oz eʔ

59 ɬɔ́ʔs ə mέs wae eʔ wəz guʌ́ɷen áoʔ so e sεz jɪ́ɷ ɬɪ́ɷʔ t'έɹəbɬ

60 | stʃə́:pɐb mán

You look awful so I cut it to make it look better because
it looked a mess while it was growing out so he says you
look terrible / Stupid man!

61 ʔʃáoʔs | e wʌ̃ɷ̃ʔ éʔ me e wʌ̃ɷ̃ʔ ɸ́:ʔ έnebade em

He shouts / He won't hit me he won't hurt anybody him.

62 jeð θέŋk o έɪz | dεʊ ʋɔ́f boʔ eɪ έznʔ ez zə mʌɷs wέɪkes lέkɬ

63 θέŋg̃

You'd think, oh he's / dead rough but he isn't he's the
most weakest little thing.

(iv) *The transcription of speaker N*

64 dáɷn t̚ sέllə | n ənoðə wan em peɪtəz bέd'ɹoum | ðáʔ wũ we

65 ád ət̚ bókstən ɹɔ́:d | ðáʔ wan op em pέɪtəz bέdɹoum wɸ́:k

66 ɔ:ɹáeʔ| eɪ fέdɬz əbǽɷʔ | t'έ:ks θέ:ɹeəɬ | jə sέɪ ɐ wɸ́:k oɸ

67 ən έndoəɹ έ:ɹeəɬ ən eʔs vέɹe kɹέtecl wέ: jə gέʔ ðe έ:ɹeəɬ |

68 gεt et en ə pɹɑ́pə spáʔ fʋɪ em tə gέt ə god̚ pέktʃə naʔ | goz

69 m pɔ́tz eʔ dǽɷn əm pɔ́ʔs eʔ sómwε:ɹ έɬs | e k'ǽ:ŋʔ gεɹ ə gób̚

70 pέktʃə

Down the cellar / and another one in Peter's bedroom / That
one we had at Buxton Road / That one up in Peter's bedroom
works alright / He fiddles about / takes the aerial / You
see I work up an indoor aerial and it's very critical where
you get the aerial / get it in a proper spot for him to get
a good picture and that / Goes and pulls it down and puts
it somewhere else / He can't get a good picture.

71 nέks dóə bəʔ wán ʃez póʔ θɹέɪ pέ:ɹ əʋ pó:ɬəɹɔed̚ ɹlásez en

72 nə bέn ən ə pέ:ɹ ə njúu ʃúuz bjúutefɬ pέ:ɹ ə ʃúuz | ən ə

36

73 pέ:ɹ ə njúu slǎks | en ʔ dósben

Next door but one she's put three pair of polaroid glasses
in the bin and a pair of new shoes, beautiful pair of
shoes / and a pair of new slacks / in the dustbin.

74 ᵊdó:nʔ θέŋk ɐv έvə bó:t ɛne

I don't think I've ever bought any.

75 wɨ lǎʔ pέ:ɹ opstέ:z ɐ fǽɷn ném ɑn | sǽɷθse béɪtʃ | pέ:ɹ ə

76 wǎ:ʔ ɹémd wónz ze ǎ: jə no: | ɐ gɑ́t ə pέ:ɹ ə ðέm əz góz

77 ensǎ:d jə ó:nɲɹe glasez̥ | ǎ: spέʃɨess sé: | jə ʃóɲɲʔ wέ:ɹ

78 əm

Well that pair upstairs I found them on / Southsea beach /
Pair of white-rimmed ones they are you know / I got a pair
of them as goes inside your ordinary glasses / Eye specialists say / you shouldn't wear them.

79 wǿ:ks ɑfʔ kǎ: bɑ́t'ɹe | ɑɹ etɨ wǿ:k ɑfʔ mé:nz | eɪ móks

80 əbǽɷʔ we ðǎʔ

Works off the car battery / or it'll work off the mains /
He mucks about with that.

81 eɪ dóz ez ó:lez móken əbǽɷʔ bénden ʔθέ:ɹeəɨ

He does, he's always mucking about bending the aerial.

82 jə nó: wət ə wəz lésnen túu ó:ɨ θɹúu | tʃəkɑ́fskez̥ féfθ

You know what I was listening to all through? /
Tchaikovsky's Fifth.

83 ɐ wəz zέ:ɹ ɑm me ó:ŋ kwǎ:ʔ lä:k | ʔsnɑ́ʔ bäd mjúuzek˥

I was there on my own quiet like / It's not bad music.

84 az e ʃó:n jə ʔ benɑ́kəɨəz e gɑ́ʔ æɒt ə tésko:

Has he shown you the binoculars he got out of Tesco?

85 nɑʔ spó:s ʔ beɪ

Not supposed to be.

86 ä dó:nʔ no wɑ́ʔ jə bó:ʔ ðέm θéŋ fɑ ðɛ nó: gód˥

I don't know what you bought them things for, they're no good.

87 ə tʃéɪp˥ pέ:ɹ ə benɑ́kjə⅃əz

A cheap pair of binoculars.

88 sótʃ əz zɑ́ʔ wɑ́nted˥ pɑ́enten æɒt˥ tə ðɑ́ʔ blɔ́:k˥ tˁoðə nɑ́:t o

89 əz ɑ́:gjen əbæɒʔ bɹéteʃ kɑ́:z ən sǿ:ves │ et éznt̚ bɹéteʃ

90 kɑ́:z əz fɔ́:lz dɑ́on │ sə mótʃ │ fɑ́ɹen kɑ́:z dɔ́z et̚

Such as that wanted pointing out to that bloke the other
night, who was arguing about British cars and service / It
isn't British cars as falls down / so much / foreign cars
does it.

91 ə dέlekət ə: enst'ɹókʃəm b⅃uk ɑn ...

A delicate er instruction book on ...

92 jə gέt só: məne stj⅃udnts ɑn fɑ́ɹen lέŋgwədʒez dɔ́ĩʔ jə │ ə

93 koəs fɹénʃ ö be ðə fǿ:s wɑ́n

You get so many students on foreign languages, don't you? /
Of course French'll be the first one.

(v) *Phonological discussion*
Inventory and distinction characteristics of the
Stockport system are negative ones in comparison to
several of the other accents presented in this book.
The most important features are: no /o/-/ʌ/ distinction, no /h/, no post-vocalic [r] before another
consonant, no /n/-/ŋ/ distinction. [ŋ] without a
following [g] occurs before another consonant as a
product of CCS (cf. Lodge, 1966 and 1981, and below
for further discussion; see also Knowles, 1978: 85).
Informant N has a vocalic distinction which Y does
not: /e:/-/ɛe/(¹), as in *wait/weight* respectively.
(This is not in the recorded material, but see Lodge,
1973.) The phonetic realization of /ae/ varies somewhat for both informants. N has a long monophthong,
[ä:] *eye* (77), which has the retracted tongue position of some realizations of /a:/, e.g. [kˁä:ŋʔ]
can't (69), or he has a diphthong [ae], as in [ɔ:ɹaeʔ]
alright (66); Y has similar realizations, e.g. [t'a:m]
time (12), [ʋaeʔ] *right* (6), but the former is kept
phonetically distinct from /ɐ:/ in terms of lip position (see (ii) above). Short vowels other than /ə/
and /e/ occur in unstressed syllables.

/r/ is realized as [ɹ] by N, but mostly as [ʋ]
by Y, though [ɹ] is used as a link sometimes and
occurs after /θ/, e.g. [pɛːɹ eɪtʃ] *pair each* (15)
and [θɹeɪ] *three* (15). There is one example of a
flap as a link: [ðɛɾ ɑːɫ] *they're all* (30).
The distribution and occurrence of [ʔ] is of
particular interest. (For some discussion, see the
Introduction.) For Y it is the realization of /t/ in
word-final position, before tautosyllabic obstruents
and in syllable-final position before all non-syllabic
consonants, e.g. [gɑʔ] *got* (8), [eʔs] *it's* (13), [eʔ
lɪɒʔ] *it look* (58). Before syllabic /l/, however,
we find [t]: compare [ʋat'ɬz] *rattles* (40) and [wɛeʔn̩]
waiting (39). Occasionally, Y uses intervocalic [ʔ]
within a word, e.g. [bɛʔə] *better* (41). She also uses
it as the realization of /k/ in word-final position,
utterance-finally and before consonants, especially
in *like*, e.g. (12), and before /t/ within a word,
e.g. [neʔt] *nicked* (16). Glottal reinforcement is
likewise widespread in her speech. (Her habits in
this respect are in line with those of group A, as
described in the Introduction.)
N, on the other hand, uses it only as a realization of syllable-final /t/ before consonants,
whether word-final or not, and in glottal reinforcement. The major difference between the two speakers
is use of [ʔ] for the definite article. Y uses it
only sporadically: [ʔtel] *the till* (22) (cf. also
[ʔ˞las] *the last* from Lodge, 1978: 67, line 119).
However, in both instances the preceding sound is [ʔ],
so that they could be interpreted as a conditioned
variant of /ð/, cf. [lae? ?a̰ʔ] *like that* (19), with
the subsequent operation of UVD, cf. [ð dosbemmen]
the dustbi nmen (15). N, on the other hand, uses it
regularly, though not exclusively, with alternant
forms depending on the environment. *The* has the
variant forms of most accents: [ðə] + C, [ðe] + V,
with consonantal harmony applying to the initial
consonant as described in Lodge (1981). The distribution of the other forms is as follows:

[t]	[ʔ]/[t̯]	[θ]
[t'oðə] (88)	[daɒn t̯ sɛllə] (64)	[θ ɛːɹeəɬ] (66)
	[en ʔ dosben] (73)	[ʔθ ɛːɹeəɬ] (81)
	[af ʔ kä:] (79)	
	[af ʔ meːnz] (79)	
	[jə ʔ benak̯ətəz] (84)	

Thus, we have the exceptional form with [t'] only in
the other (though a form [θ oðə], not recorded here,

is also used in Stockport, cf. SED III: 1065); before consonants we have [ʔ] with a simultaneous alveolar closure between alveolar sounds; before vowels [θ], though following continuants and vowels the form is [ʔθ]. (There are no recorded examples of the latter in the material I am using; an example would be: [fə ʔθ ɛːɹeəɬ] *for the aerial*.)

The question as to what the underlying form is is somewhat complex. If /t/ is chosen, since it is the phonological element to which most occurrences of [ʔ] are related, we have its regular realization, mostly without oral closure, in syllable-final position, the vowel of the article being deleted first by UVD. In this case we have the derivation as in (1).

(1)   /ɑf tV meːnz/([2])

    Stress placement   ⇒   ɑf tə méːnz

    UVD   ⇒   ɑf t méːnz

    /t/-realization   ⇒   [ɑf ʔ méːnz]

(I have left the intermediate stages of the derivation without brackets to indicate that their exact phonological status is undetermined. For some discussion of intermediate status, specifically related to SPE, see Fudge, 1967.) The prevocalic instances involve the addition of [θ] and, after obstruents, the deletion of [t]. We thus have the derivations (2) and (3).

(2)   /teːks tV ɛːɹeəl/

    Stress placement   ⇒   téːks tə ɛ́ːɹeəl

    UVD   ⇒   téːks t ɛ́ːɹeəl

    θ-insertion   ⇒   téːks tθ ɛ́ːɹeəl

    CCS   ⇒   [teːks θ ɛ́ːɹeəɬ]

(3)   /-en tV ɛːɹeəl/

    Stress placement   ⇒   -en tə ɛ́ːɹeəl

    UDV   ⇒   -en t ɛ́ːɹeəl

    θ-insertion   ⇒   -en tθ ɛ́ːɹeəl

    /t/-realization   ⇒   [-en ʔθ ɛ́ːɹeəɬ]

CCS does not apply to /t/ after nasals (cf. Lodge, 1981: 34).

The main problem with this solution is the unmotivated θ-insertion rule; it is *ad hoc* to this particular lexical item. Furthermore, there is no

40

obvious relationship between these forms and the
forms with initial /ð/. An alternative solution
would be to posit an underlying /θV/ for the article.
This would indicate more clearly the relationship
with /ðV/([3]), giving speakers the option of a "voiced"
or a "voiceless" article, depending on certain social
considerations. (The factors determining this choice
are unclear to me, but include sex of the speaker,
sex of the hearer(s), and their perceived social
status.) The rules involved would then be:

(1')   /ɑf θV meːnz/

 Stress placement ⇒ ɑf θə méːnz

 UVD ⇒ ɑf θ méːnz

 t-insertion ⇒ ɑf tθ méːnz

 CCS ⇒ ɑf t méːnz

 /t/-realization ⇒ [ɑf ʔ méːnz]

(2')   /teːks θV ɛːɹeəl/

 Stress placement ⇒ téːks θə ɛ́ːɹeəl

 UVD ⇒ [téːks θ ɛ́ːɹeəɫ]

(3')   /-en θV ɛːɹeəl/

 Stress placement ⇒ -en θə ɛ́ːɹeəl

 UVD ⇒ -en θ ɛ́ːɹeəl

 t-insertion ⇒ -en tθ ɛ́ːɹeəl

 /t/-realization ⇒ [-en ʔθ ɛ́ːɹeəɫ]

This is preferable to the analysis as /tV/ because
of the clearer representation of the relationship
with /ðV/ and the avoidance of the *ad hoc* rule of θ-
insertion. The t-insertion rule, on the other hand,
represents part of a general insertion phenomenon,
stop epenthesis, which has operated at various times
throughout the history of English (eg. the /b/ in
thimble, /d/ in *thunder*, etc. cf. Strang, 1970: 166,
and Anderson and Jones, 1977: 130). In (1') the rule
deleting θ can either be seen as an extension of CCS
(which applies elsewhere, too, e.g. in words such as
fifths, *sixths* and *months*), or as a simplification
of an otherwise impossible syllable-initial cluster
θ + obstruent.
 In either solution the one remaining problem is
absolute initial [ʔ] before consonants (no examples
recorded), as in [ʔ bos ez komen] *The bus is coming.*

This cannot be accounted for by the rules given
so far, but since the available material is insufficient to give a proper analysis, I shall leave
this unanswered here, though I shall return to this
problem in the last chapter(⁴).
There is a constraint on the occurrence of [ˀ]
for both informants: a sequence ˀV̆, where V̆ =
unstressed vowel, either [ə] or [e], is ruled out,
except in absolute initial sequences with an added
glottal onset, as in [ˀeˀs] (27). Thus, we find
[ént̚ eˀ] *isn't it?* (27), but not *[énˀ eˀ](⁵).
I shall now turn to the phonological processes,
which are more widespread in Y's than in N's speech.

(a) *Lenition*. The most common lenition in Stockport
is stop → fricative (cf. Lodge, 1981: 20-22):

[peɪɸo] *people* (13)

[n̥ə βos] *the bus* (26)

[puesɛnd] *pretend* (28)

[ɐ ɣo] *I go* (33)

[tox eˀ] *took it* (56)

[oɸ ən] *up an* (66-67).

The other lenition process, which occurs quite often,
is the vocalization or even deletion of /l/, e.g.

[nʌɷ ɣaek] *know like* (36)

[gɪɣ fuɛnd] *girl friend* (45)

[wae eˀ] *while it* (59).

There are no examples of this in N's speech.

(b) *Harmony*. Consonantal harmony is widespread in
Y's speech, less so in N's (see Lodge, 1981, for a
detailed discussion of this process in Stockport).
It is the alveolar series, /t d n s z/, in particular,
which harmonize in preconsonantal position to the
place of articulation of the following consonant, e.g.

[tɛm mene?] *ten-minute* (18)

[fefteɪm pɛns] *fifteen pence* (27)

[soŋ ʋae?] *some right* (29)

[aṇ ṇə] *on the* (26)

[job̚ bɛ?ə] *you'd better* (41)

[sɛd̥ ðə] *said the* (38)

[woǯ̚ ko?] *wood-cut* (35)

[oːŋ kwäː?] *own quiet* (83)

[gobˈ pektʃə] *good picture* (69-70).

Note that in N's case harmony is not so consistently applied as by Y: [godˈ pektʃə] also occurs in line (68). In the case of /t/ the realizations are found both with and without supraglottal closure:

[ɑpəzepˈ búeteʃ] *opposite British* (23)

[kədɛ? kɑːs] *cadet course* (7).

In the case of /-nd/ and /-nt/ the harmony applies to both segments, e.g.

[paoŋψ fefte] *pound fifty* (20)

[dom? bɑðə] *doesn't bother* (53)

[wɛŋ? fə] *went for* (5) and (7)

[woʈ? geβ] *wouldn't give* (9).

(In the case of /-nt/ the supraglottal closure is held throughout the glottal one.)
Syllabic /n/ often harmonizes with the preceding consonant, e.g.

[ʌɶpm̩d] *opened* (10)

[buɛeǩ ʈ] *break and* (13).

Palatalization of /t d s z/ occurs before /j/. /s/ is most consistently palatalized; there are exceptions for /d/ and /z/, e.g.

[ʃɛ?ʃe] *shakes you* (49)

[maend³ jɪɶ] *mind you* (31)

[dɛd joŋ] *dead young* (30)

[sɛz jɪɶ] *says you* (59).

Some examples involve CCS (see next section) as well as harmony, e.g.

[nɛçʃ jeə] *next year* (1)

[kɑʃₒᵉ] *costs you* (26).

Word-initial [ʃ] also produces harmony in the appropriate preceding consonant (for details, see Lodge, 1981: 27-28), e.g.

[doʒ̥ ʃe] *does she* (52).

With /t/, which is realized mostly as [?] in word-final position, no harmony can take place, e.g.

[gɛ? je] *get your* (32).

Occasionally harmony occurs within a word, e.g.
[stʃəːp̯e̯b] *stupid* (60).

N has two palatal articulations, which may be interpreted as instances of harmony, not found in Y's speech,

[kɹetecl̩] *critical* (67)

[poːɫəɹɔedˀ ɟlasez] *polaroid glasses* (71).

He also uses a velar articulation, as in:

[ɔːnɲɹe glasez] *ordinary glasses* (77).

From these examples it is difficult to see exactly what the conditioning environment is, though it is probably the place of articulation of the preceding sound (bearing in mind that the final vowel of *ordinary* is centralized because it is unstressed, whereas the unstressed vowel in *critical* is not centralized, perhaps under the influence of the stressed [e]). We may note further that a number of speakers in the Stockport area have such articulations for /kl/ and /gl/ and that the exact point of contact on the roof of the mouth for /l/-realizations and the posture of the rest of the tongue varies quite a lot depending on the surrounding sounds (cf. Lodge, 1978: 61).

Another kind of place harmony is to be found only in Y's speech, as can be seen from the alternation of bilabial and labiodental articulations, e.g.

[geβ me] *give me* (9)

[faːβ pɛns] *five pence* (20) and (26)

[stoɸ wɛeʔʨ] *stuff waiting* (38-39)

[a·β beŋ] *I've been* (42).

In addition Y also displays a tendency to harmonize consonants to a labiodental place of articulation even when there are intervening vowels, e.g.

[gʊɛeψ ʋɑn] *grade one* (1)

[tɛʋəψo] *terrible* (27)

[ʋeəɫe ʋɑz] *really was* (4).

In the last example there is also an intervening lingual consonant, but this does not affect the labiodental posture. (For a discussion of this in relation to child language, see Lodge, 1983, and cf. Stampe's comments on non-contiguous harmony, 1979: 76.) A particularly striking example of labiodental harmony is:

[ɐ kɛπ ŋe ɛψ kovəd oπ fəʊ ɛedʒez]

I kept my head covered up for ages (57).

This could be seen as a "left-over" from the acquisition period. The dentals /θ/ and /ð/ harmonize with alveolar fricatives both before and after them (cf. Lodge, 1981: 29). There are no examples of /θ/ in the texts in this position, only of /ð/, e.g.

[eʔs zə] *it's the* (24)

[senəməz zɛ:] *cinemas there* (24)

[əz zaʔ] *as that* (88).

We shall consider /ð/ further below.

The other main type of harmony, that of manner (in addition to place harmony in most cases), is only found in Y's speech, e.g.

[waw̃ʔ wø:ken] *wasn't working* (46)

[lɪɒkeʊ ʋa:ʔ] *looking right* (25)

[doʊ̃ʔ ʋɛk̂ʈ] *don't reckon* (17)

[waɪ̃ lɐd] *one lad* (44)

[ə̃j̃ jə] *and you're* (25).

Although the sound most commonly affected is /n/, we also find manner harmony with /m l ð/ and occasionally the oral stops, too, e.g.

[aṇ ṇə] *on the* (26)

[ɐw̃ watʃen] *I'm watching* (33-34)

[a:ʋ ʋa:ʔ] *all right* (45)

[a:ɫ lə] *all the* (12)

[laeʔ ʔa̰ʔ] *like that* (19)

[lað fə] *lad for* (42)

[nɛçʃ] *next* (1)

[dʒaβ ðɛ̃] *job then* (6)

[dɛʋ ʋof] *dead rough* (62).

With the exception of /ð/→[ʔ] 'and [ṇ], these examples of manner harmony follow the direction of lenition, that is, stops become fricatives or frictionless continuants, but not the other way round.

In one instance /d/ has harmonized as to place and nasality, giving: [tʌɒɫm me] *told me* (38).

45

Harmony of nasality only also occurs but is not common:

[ʌɒpn̩ ð̃e] *open they* (21)

[depɛnnz] *depends* (51).

There is also an example of vocalization of syllabic /l/:

[peɪɸo wɛn] *people when* (13),

which could also be the explanation for the vocalization of initial /l/ in *know like*, given above under lenition.

(c) *CCS*. Consonantal cluster simplification applies to both speakers. There are several examples from Stockport given in the Introduction and I shall not repeat them here. They affect /t/ and /d/ interconsonantally. Some of the examples also involve harmony, and we find both unsimplified and simplified clusters with harmony. Consider the following:

/paond fefte/

Place Harmony ⇒ [-ŋψ f-]

/seɪmd tə/

CCS ⇒ [-m tə]

/and pots/

Place Harmony ⇒ -mb p-

CCS ⇒ [-m p-].

The situation is somewhat different for /n/ before /t/: it is the /n/ that is deleted whether there are consonants following /t/ or not, e.g. [wɑ? ə] *want a* (54). However, it is common for the nasality to remain, as in [wʌɒ̃? ø̃:?] *won't hurt* (61), [doĩ? jə] *don't you* (92). Nasal harmony followed by /n/-deletion (cf. Hyman's discussion of French, 1975: 130-31) will only account for the forms with nasalized vowels; the non-nasal forms would require a further nasality-deletion rule, optional before /t/. On the other hand, if the rules can apply in either order, the non-nasalized forms would be accounted for by /n/-deletion alone.

In the sequence /ng/ the /n/ behaves differently in the unstressed endings /-eng/ and /-θeng/ from elsewhere, including stressed /θeng/. Thus, we find [komen] *coming* (32), [somθen] *something* (40), [θeŋg̊]

46

thing (63) and [θeŋz] *things* (36). In the last two
examples the nasal is velar, i.e. it has harmonized
with the following /g/, deleted by CCS in *things*.
In the first two examples, though, we have an alveolar nasal. Furthermore, this unstressed -*ing* ending
shows the place harmonies displayed by /n/, e.g.

[wɑtʃeŋ̊ n̥ə] (34)

[wɛeʔm̥ fə] (39)

[somθel̃ laeʔ] (53).

We thus need to distinguish the -*(th)ing* endings from
the other occurrences of /-ng/. In the latter case
the /n/ is subject to velar harmony, then CCS applies
to delete the /g/, when there is a following consonant,
e.g.

/θengz/

Place Harmony	⇒	θeŋgz
CCS	⇒	[θeŋz] (36).

In absolute final position, where CCS does not apply,
the /g/ sometimes is deleted, but not always; thus,
[θeŋg̊] (63), but [joŋ] (30). There is also fluctuation within a word; compare [eŋɫəʃ] (51) with
[eŋgleʃ] (1). This example seems to indicate a
fluctuation in syllable structure; CCS only applies
to a stop articulation in the coda of a syllable, so
the former example must have the boundary after the
/g/, whereas the latter one has it before the /g/.
    With the unstressed endings there are two possi-
bilities. They may behave exactly like stressed
/-eng/, e.g.

/-eng t-/

Place Harmony	⇒	-eŋg t-
CCS	⇒	[-eŋ t-] (4).

Otherwise /g/ is deleted before any harmony takes
place, e.g.

/-eng l-/

/g/-deletion	⇒	-en l-
Manner Harmony	⇒	[-el̃ l-] (53).

This is not CCS, because the same deletion takes
place before a vowel, e.g. [goen aœʔ] *going out* (42)
(⁶).
    Finally, we may note that there are more complex
derivations, as follows:

```
                    /-eng ʊ-/
/g/-deletion        ⇒    -en ʊ-
Place Harmony       ⇒    -eŋ ʊ-
Manner Harmony      ⇒    [-eũ ʊ-] (25)

                    /-ɛkst j-/
CCS                 ⇒    -ɛks j-
Place Harmony       ⇒    -ɛkʃ j-
Manner Harmony      ⇒    [-ɛçʃ j-] (1).
```

There are two late, optional rules, which can
apply after CCS and Harmony, as exemplified by the
following instance:

```
                    /-sts j-/
CCS                 ⇒    -ss j-
Place Harmony       ⇒    -ʃʃ j-
Geminate Simplif.   ⇒    -ʃ j-
/j/-deletion        ⇒    [-ʃ°ᵉ] (26).
```

Palatal harmony applies to all identical preceding
alveolars (cf. Lodge, 1981: 37). Geminate Simplification and /j/-deletion are characteristic of rapid
speech. The former applies to all such sound
sequences, e.g. [ɑː ɫə] *all the* (49), though it is
optional as demonstrated by [spɛʃɫess seː] *specialists say* (77). The latter rule applies after [ʃ]
and [ʒ] across a word- or syllable-boundary, when
the word with initial /j/ is unstressed, cf. also
[ʃɛeʔʃe] *shakes you* (49).

(d) *UVD.* The circumstances under which this rule
applies are difficult to determine in any general
way. It is optional and not applied regularly. The
commonest occurrence is loss of initial unstressed
vowels, especially in absolute initial position or
after vowels, e.g.

[so m] *so I'm* (1)

[sɛɸ̞] *except* (2)

[govə] *go over* (19)

[ʔtʃɛendʒ] *I changed* (31)

[ʃɛeʔʃe baɶʔ] *shakes you about* (49)

[ʔdepɛnnz] *it depends* (51)

[ʔʃaoʔs] *He shouts* (61)

[goz] *He goes* (68)

[ʔs] *It's* (83).

A preceding glottal stop also appears to bring about
the loss of an unstressed vowel, e.g.

[stɑʔpɔəʔ ʔs] *Stockport that's* (10)

[eʔ~b] *it would* (39)

[aeʔ ʔə] *out of the* (55)

[spo:s ʔ beɪ] *suppǫsed to be* (85).

See also above for the treatment of the glottal stop
as the definite article, where UVD is involved.
The unstressed auxiliary verbs, *an*, *and* and *not*
in particular can lose their syllabicity when the
surrounding sounds are vowels or semi-vowels (/j/ and
/w/), e.g. [ewznəp-] (37), with two syllables rather
than four, and [wɒnʔ] *wasn't* (8) alongside [wɒnʔ] (7).
The other main instances of UVD are those'discussed in the Introduction, where CV́CəCə is reduced
to CV́CCə, where C = at least one consonant, and the
final vowel may also be [e], e.g.

[əpʌɒɫstʋə] *upholsterer* (37)

[batʼɹe] *battery* (79).

(e) *Linking r*. Both informants use linking r exten-
sively, but not on every occasion where it might
apply, e.g.

[ðɛ: ə̃j̃] *there and* (25)

[jə ɔ:nnɹe] *your ordinary* (77).

Y uses [ʋ], [ɹ] and [ɾ] as links, the former being
the most common. The link only occurs after [ə],
[ɐ:] (or [ä:]), [ø:] and [ɔ:] (or [ɑ:])(⁷).

NOTES

1. For one possible interpretation of the
Stockport diphthongs, see Lodge (1973).
2. The precise nature of the underlying vowel
phase of the article is not important here; V represents some kind of full vowel.
3. On the history of the definite article, see,
for example, Strang (1970). The historical relationship would also be captured in this analysis. The
[θ]~[ð] (Strang, ibid.: 181) alternations could perhaps also be incorporated by means of realization
rules operating on one underlying dental fricative

(cf. Fudge, 1969b: 271), but I shall not pursue this
further here.

⁴. For a considerable amount of raw data,
presented without any analysis, the reader is referred
to the SED. In Stockport, before vowels [θ] is used
in absolute initial position; before most consonants
[ʔ] is used, though in the case of frictionless
continuants, both can occur.

⁵. It is worth noting that this is a right-to-
left constraint and is evidence for "advance planning"
of articulatory moves in speech (cf. Hardcastle, 1981
and refs.). There is a similar constraint in Norwich
(Trudgill, 1974: 174-75).

⁶. The /g/-deletion is *ad hoc* to these forms
only, unlike in some of the other accents presented
in this book. Historically the participle ending in
/n/ has a different origin from that ending in /ng/
(cf. Strang, 1970: 238). It would be possible, therefore, to have two alternative participial forms, one
with /-n/, the other with /-ng/, avoiding the need
for a separate /g/-deletion rule. The unstressed
-*thing* ending would also have to be given these
alternative forms, even though they are historically
not justified in this case. This could be seen as
an analogical spread from the participles.

⁷. It is possible that there are circumstances
where a link would never be used, but there is no
evidence of this in the extracts. In *Shaw Heath*,
for example, I have never heard a link used. This
may be explained by the fact that in older forms of
Stockport speech the first word would have had a
back closing diphthong (cf. the Introduction, above),
which would not allow a link anyway.

Chapter Two

SHEPHERD'S BUSH, LONDON, W12

There is one informant, C, aged 60. She was born in
Shepherd's Bush, moved to Northolt in 1938, and to
Norfolk in 1970. There has been no noticeable
adoption of any Norfolk pronunciations. A comparison
with Cockney pronunciation shows up a number of
differences (see, for example, Wells, 1982: 301-34).

(i) *General*
Most stops have a complete closure, though there is a
tendency to produce flaps in intervocalic position.
In the release phase only [t] is ever affricated. A
slight amount of creaky voice is sometimes to be
heard in the vicinity of a glottal stop. The lips
are rounded by slight protrusion of the lips with a
corresponding drawing in at the sides. Non-rounded
lip positions are either spread or neutral, depending
on the stress of the syllable in question.

(ii) *Vowel diagrams*

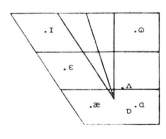

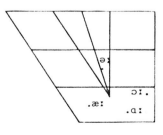

short stressed　　　　　long stressed

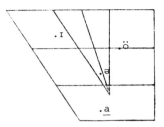

unstressed

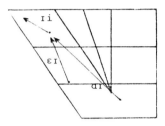

front closing diphthongs
(No examples of [ɔɪ].)

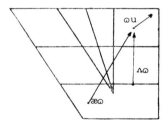

back closing diphthongs

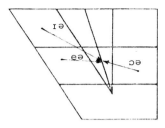

centring diphthongs

Unstressed vowels have neutral lip position, except
for [ö] and [ɷ] which have no lip protrusion but
drawn-in sides.

(iii) *The transcription*

1 ɑɪ ɔ́:wɪʒ jɷ́us t'æv mɑ́ɪn ᶦʔjɷ́us tə fɔ́:ö ðǽʔ wέɪ | ðǽʔs ɔ́:ö

2 kʌ́mɪŋ bǽk næɷ ʃʌ́ɷdə lέn̥θ heə ən ɪʔ sέd jə nʌ́ɷ nɪ́idˈ tə hæv |

3 a̠ θɪŋk a̠v stɪ́ö gɑ́ʔ ðə p'έɪpəɹ a̠ wəz̥ gʌ́ɷnə bɹɪ́ŋ ɪʔ ɹɑ́ɷn:

4 bət ɑɪ dʒʌs kɷ́dn̩ʔ pɷ́ʔ ma̠ hǽ:nd ɒn ɪʔ | ɪʔs mɔ́:ɹ ə lέs ðə

5 stɑ́ɪö wɒʔ ðɛɪ jɷ́us t'æv | dʒʌs ðɪ έ:ndˈ tέ:nd ʌ́p ə bɪtˀ

I always used to have mine - it used to fall that way /
that's all coming back now shoulder-length hair and it said
you no need to have / I think I've still got the paper I
was going to bring it round but I just couldn't put my hand
on it / it's more or less the style what they used to have
/ Just the end turned up a bit.

6 wɛl a̠ dʌ́ɷ̃ʔ θɪ̃ʔ mɑ́ɪ̃z vɛɹɪi mɑ́:vɫəs ɪz ɪʔ ɹɹi³ɫɹi ɑɪ dənʌ́ɷ

Well, I don't think mine's very marvellous is it really?
I don't know.

7 wɛɫ lɪ ʌ́ðə wɪ́ik ɑɪ dʒʌs kɷ́dnt̚ dɒu ə θɪ́ŋ wɪ́ð ɪd ɪʔ sɪɪnd

8 ʔǽbsəlɷ́uʔtlɪi hʌ́ɷplɪs | bəʔ sætədɛɪ ɪʔ sɪ́im tə dʒəs gʌ́ɷ

9 ʔɹ́izəɫɪ əʒ jou wɷ́ntəd ɛ̥t

Well, the other week I just couldn't do a thing with it, it

53

seemed absolutely hopeless / but Saturday it seemed to just
go easily as you wanted it.

10 jə gɛ́ʔ sʌm ínɛkspɹíiˀ̕ɹɪənsst wʌnz a̲ səpˈʌ̃ʊz
⠀⠀⠀ ⠀You get some inexperienced ones I suppose.

11 a̲ θĩ́ʔ ðɛɪ dʒʌ́s gʌ̃ʊ tɐ ə ʃʊ̃pˀ dʌ̃ʊ̃ʔ ðɛɪ | ðǽʔs wɒt ɑɪ θĩ́ŋk

12 əbaⱷp maɪ sʌ́nz wɑ́ɪf | bɪkɒ ʃɪz gɒʔ nʌ̃ʊ sətɪ́fɪkɪts əɹ

13 ɛ́nɪθɪŋʔ fə héədɹɛsɪŋ əɹ ɛ́nɪθɪŋ au̯̰ ʃɔ́:ᵊ ðæʔs wɒʔ ʃɹ́i mʌ́st

14 əv dʌ́n
⠀⠀⠀ ⠀I think they just go to a shop, don't they? / That's what
⠀⠀⠀ ⠀I think about my son's wife / because she's got no certif-
⠀⠀⠀ ⠀icates or anything for hairdressing or anything I'm sure
⠀⠀⠀ ⠀that's what she must have done.

15 nʌ́:ⱷ a̲ səpʌ̃ʊ | ðɛ θĩ́ŋk ʌ̃ʊɛl ɪˀs ə pɛ̰́:m ən ɪ ˀs tɑ́ɪdɪ ən̰ n̰ǽʔs

16 ɹ́t
⠀⠀⠀ ⠀No, I suppose / they think, oh well it's a perm and it's
⠀⠀⠀ ⠀tidy and that's it.

17 bʌ̰ʔ ðɛ wɒ́z əm ə tɔ́:k sʌm wɑ́ɪɫ əgʌ̃ʊ əbáⱷʔ ðɹ́iz pɹ́ɪpɫ hǽvɪŋ

18 tˈⱷu gʌ̃ʊ | jə nʌ̃ʊ ɫ lɹiz héədɹɛsɪŋ pɹ́ɪpɫ stˈɑ́:tɪŋ ʌ̃ɸ ʔ hʌ̃ʊm

19 ən ɔ́:ɫ lɹ́s bɹ́znɪs
⠀⠀⠀ ⠀But there was m a talk some while ago about these people
⠀⠀⠀ ⠀having to go / you know all these hairdressing people
⠀⠀⠀ ⠀starting up at home and all this business.

20 kⱷz jⱷv gɒ́ʔ nʌ̃ʊ klɛ́ɪm ɒn̰ n̰əm ǽv jⱷu ɒɹ ɛ́nɪθɪŋ ɪf sʌ́mθɪŋ

21 hǽpmn̄d ɪf ðɛɪ gɛ́ɪv jⱷu ə pɛ̰́:m ən ɪʔ ɹ́ⱷuɪndʒə héə wɛ wⱷ́ʔ

22 kⱷdʒə dⱷ́u | jⱷ wⱷ́n̰ æv ə lɛ̃́gˀ tə stǽ:nd ɒn wⱷ́dʒö ɹɪ́:əɫɪ |

23 ðǽ:ʔs sə tɹʌ́bö
⠀⠀⠀ ⠀Cos you've got no claim on them, have you, or anything if
⠀⠀⠀ ⠀something happened if they gave you a perm and it ruined
⠀⠀⠀ ⠀your hair, well what could you do? / You wouldn't have a
⠀⠀⠀ ⠀leg to stand on, would you, really? / That's the trouble.

24 sʌ́m pɹ́ɪpɫ ðɛɪ wö wⱷ́n̰ʔ n̰ɹ́s dʌ́n | ɹɹ́ɪlɪ ɪˀs sɛɹ ʌ̃ʊĩ ɹɪ́sk ën̰

25 eʔ ɪf ðɛɪ ǽv vɹiz θɪŋz dʌ́n
⠀⠀⠀ ⠀Some people they, well, want this done / really it's their
⠀⠀⠀ ⠀own risk, isn't it, if they have these things done?

26 dɑ́:k⁾ ˀpɾíɸö gʌ◌ɪŋ blʊ́nd

Dark people going blond.

27 jéː°s sɛɪ k'ɑ́:mp⁾ bɪ bʊ́ðəd ◌ səpʌ◌z
＋ ◌
Yes, they can't be bothered I suppose.

28 ɪˀ lǒks əz ɪf ʃɪz ǽd̥ ðə pɛ́ɪnˀpɒt ʊ́n ɪˀ ɔ́: lə tɑ́ɪm ən a̲
29 wʌ́ndə wɒˀɛ́vəɹ ɪˀs gʌ◌nə dǒu tə hə̰: skɪ́n lɛɪt'ɹ ʊ́n kɾ́ip⁾
30 pʊ́tɪŋ ɔ́: læˀ stʌ́f ɒn | ɪts ɹɪdɪ́kjʊləs ɹɪ́ilɹi ɑɪ θɪ́ŋk̚ məsɛ́öf

It looks as if she's had the paint-pot on it all the time
and I wonder whatever it's going to do to her skin later on
keep putting all that stuff on / It's ridiculous really I
think myself.

31 dʒö mémbə sǽtədɛɪ wɛw̃ wɪ wə k'ʌ́mɪŋ ʌp ðə ɹʌ◌d ɪŋ ṇə k'ɑ́: ən
32 ɑɪ sɛ́d ɑɪ θɔ́:t ɪˀ wəz ðʌ◌z: pɾ́ipö fɹəm ɾ́isbɔːn

Do you remember Saturday when we were coming up the road in
the car and I said I thought it was those people from East-
bourne?

33 ɪˀ wʊ̰z zɛ́m jö nʌ◌

It was them you know.

34 ◌ sɛd ðǽˀ lǒˀt lɑɪk̚ | ðɾ́iz̥ tǒu wɔ́:kɪw̃ wɛ ðə lɛ́ɪdɹi wəz ◌̰ ðə
＋
35 pɛ́ɪvmən ᵈ əṇ ṇə hʌ́zbənd lǒk̚ lɑɪk̚ ɪn | ɑɪ hæˀnt sɪ́in əm fɔ
36 s:ɪ́kʃ jɾ́iəz̥ | nʌ◌ kɔ́:s ɪd ɪ́znt

I said that looked like / these two walking, well, the lady
was on the pavement and the husband looked like him / I
hadn't seen them for six years / No, course it isn't.

37 ɛ́nɪwɛɪ wɪ fǎ◌ṇ ṇɪs nʌ◌t wɛw̃ wɪ gɒɾ ɪ́n

Anyway we found this note when we got in.

38 ɪˀʃ jɔ́:ᵊ hǎ◌s ɪ̰zn ɪˀ

It's your house, isn't it?

39 ◌ dɪdn ʌndəstǽːmb wɑ́ɪ ʃɪ sɛ́d ʃɪ kɵdnː ̀ lɛ́t ə: lǒk æt ɪt̚ ˀ |
＋ ◌
40 sə bɪ́ˀ sɪ́lɹi ɹɪ́ᵊlɹi | wö ðæˀs dɑ́:fp bɪkəz ɪˀs nʊ́ˀ dəzn ̀
41 bɪlʊ́ŋ tə ðɪ ɛ́ɪdʒən: ɪˀs ɛ́: ha◌s

55

I didn't understand why she said she couldn't let her look
at it / It's bit silly really / Well, that's daft, because
it's not doesn't belong to the agent, it's her house.

42 ʃɪ wɒ̃nˀtəd mɪi tə sɛ́ɳɳ ɳɪs tɛ́lɪgɹǽːm tə ðəm | waɪ aɪ ʃb

43 wɛ́ɪsˀtˀmʌ́nɪi ɒn tɛ́lɪgɹǽːmz ən θɪŋz laɪˀ ðǽːt

She wanted me to send this telegram to them / Why I should
waste money on telegrams and things like that.

44 kö̩s zə lɛ́təz̥ ədˀbɹɪŋ kɹʊ́sɪŋ ɪŋ ɳ̩ə pʌ́ɷst

'Cos the letters had been crossing in the post.

45 ɑ wəz dʒɛ́ːst jə nʌɷ dóʊɪ͡ŋ͡nə mɪ́iɫ əɳ̩ fʌ́ɷw̃ wɛ́nˀ nɛ́ks dóə ɳ̩
   +

46 ɳ̩ɛɪ kɛ́ɪm əz̃ sɛ́d ɔ ɪts fə jóu

I was just you know doing the meal and [the] phone went
next door and they came and said, Oh, it's for you.

47 dɪd vɪ́k hæv ə | sʊ́f twɪ́id hǽt ɒn ɔ sʌ́mθɪŋˀ laɪˀ lǽːˀ | wɒ

48 lókɪŋ aɷˀ ðə kǎ̩ː aɪ sɛ ɪˀ lóˀ sʌ́mθɪŋˀ laɪˀ lǽːˀ | ʃɪ sɛd wɫ

49 áɪ hæd ə bɹǽɷn pɪ́nɪfɔə dɹɛs

Did Vic have a / soft tweed hat on or something like that?
/ Well, looking out of the car, I said, it looked something
like that. / She said, Well, I had a brown pinafore dress.

50 sʌɷ ʃɪi sɛ wɪi kˀɔ́ŋˀ gɛˀ nɪi á̩ːnsə fɹəm ɳɪs háɷs

So she said, We couldn't get any answer from this house.

51 ɛ́nɪwɛɪ ʃɪ sɛd wɪi pɒπ fɪ́ftɪi pǎ̩ɷnz daɒn ɒɳ̩ ɳ̩ə lá̩ːs bʌ́ŋɡəlʌɷ

52 ðəˀs tə bɪ bɪ́ɫˀ lɛ́ə

Anyway she said, We put fifty pounds down on the last
bungalow that's to be built there.

53 ɪˀs tɪ́pɪkɫ ɒv əm ðeɹ ó̩ː lə sɛ́ɪm | nʌɷ dɪ́fɹ̩tʃˀ fəɹ ɛ́nɪwʌn

54 ɛ̈́ɫs

It's typical of them, they're all the same / No different
for anyone else.

55 sǽtədɛɪ hɪi ɹʌ́ŋ | djɷu má̩ɪnd ɪf aɪ stɛ́ɹ nɛks wɪ́ik

Saturday he rung / Do you mind if I stay next week?

56

56 mʌs bɹi dɪ́fɪkŏˀ ɹɪ́ilɹi mʌ́sn̩ ɪˀ
Must be difficult really, mustn't it?

57 wǫ̈ lɛɪ dʌ̃ŏˀ wŏ̈ˀ mɹi tə lɪ́iv jɛ́t əwɑɪɫ | θɪ́ŋk ðɛv bɪn lɪ́vɪn
58 ɪɾ ʌ́p ə bɪt̚ ðɪs lɑ́ːst wɹ́ik̚ | wɛ́nt tɷ ə kʼʌ́pl əv dɑ́ːz̃sɪz jɷ
59 nʌ̃ɷ

Well, they don't want me to leave yet awhile. / Think
they've been living it up a bit this last week. / Went to
a couple of dances, you know.

60 ðɪ́s wɹik hɹiz gʊ́t̚ tə gʌ̃ɷ tə skʊ́ˀlənd | sʌ̃θɪŋk̚ tə dɷ́u wɪ ðə
61 fǫ̈ːm

This week he's got to go to Scotland / something to do with
the firm.

62 a̲ dʌ̃ɷn wʊ́nə wʌ́ɹɪ jɷu | mɛ́ɪkɪn ə bɪ́gʼ dʒʊ́b
I don't want to worry you / making a big job.

(iv) *Phonological discussion*
The most important characteristics of C's speech are:
the /ɷ/-/ʌ/ distinction, no syllable-final /r/, consistent use of /h/, unstressed, word-final /ɪi/. [ŋ]
occurs without a following [g] more than in Stockport;
see below for details. The commonest processes are
harmony and CCS.

(a) *Lenition.* The bilabials appear to be those
sounds that are particularly subject to lenition, e.g.
    [ʌɸ] *up* (18)
    [pɹiɸö] *people* (26)
    [a̲ṵ̃] *I'm* (13).
In the last example, the lenition has gone from stop
to vocoid. There is also frequent vocalization of
/l/ in word-final or pre-consonantal position, e.g.
    [stɹö] *still* (3)
    [pɹiɸö] *people* (26)
    [pɹipö] *people* (32)
    [məsɛöf] *myself* (30).
There are, however, exceptions to this, e.g.
    [wɑɪɫ] *while* (17)

57

[pɹipɫ] *people* (17).

The other frequent type of lenition is intervocalic voicing of /t/

[ɪd ɪʔ] *it it* (7) (with partial voicing only)

[ɪd ɪznt̩] *it isn't* (36).

There is also a tendency to flap such consonants, e.g.

[gɒɾ ɪn] *got in* (37).

(b) *Harmony*. The alveolars /t d n/ harmonize their place of articulation to a following consonant, e.g.

[əbaɔp̚ maɪ] *about my* (12)

[kʼaːmp̚ bɪ] *can't be* (27)

[ʌndəstæːmb waɪ] *understand why* (39)

[daːfp̚ bɪkəz] *daft because* (40)

[ʃb wɛɪsʔt] *should waste* (42-43)

[pɔπ̚ fɪftɪi] *put fifty* (51)

[dɪfɹɧʔ fəɹ] *different for* (53)

[əbaɔt̪̚ ðɪiz̥] *about these* (17).

Although place harmony is usual, there are examples where it does not occur, e.g.

[pɛɪnʔpɒt] *paint-pot* (28).

In the case of syllabic nasals there are dual articulations, as in

[hæpmn̄d] *happened* (21).

There are also a number of examples of manner harmony, with place harmony as well, as appropriate, e.g.

[ʌɔĩ ɹɪsk] *own risk* (24)

[wɛw̃ wɪ] *when we* (31) and (37)

[əz̃ sɛd] *and said* (46).

There is a left-to-right nasal harmony of [nd]-sequences, whether /nd/ originally, or derived from /nt/ by voicing (lenition), e.g.

[ɹaɔn:] *round* (3)

[ɛɪdʒən:] *agent* (41).

58

The derivation of the latter form is thus:

/ɛɪdʒənt/

Voicing	⇒	ɛɪdʒənd
Nasal harmony	⇒	[ɛɪdʒənː].

This harmony does not always take place, as can be seen from a form such as [pɛɪvmənd] *pavement* (35). There is one context where the harmony affects two following segments: /nd ð/, as in:

/sɛnd ðɪs/

Nasal harmony	⇒	sɛnn ðɪs
ð harmony	⇒	sɛnn n̪ɪs
Place harmony	⇒	[sɛn̪n̪ n̪ɪs] (42).

In rapid speech Geminate Simplification takes place; this is particularly common with the negative ending of auxiliary verbs, e.g.

[wɒn̩] *wouldn't* (22)

[ɪzn̩] *isn't* (38).

The disappearance of the final /t/ is not caused by CCS, because such cases may be followed by either a consonant or a vowel. (The above examples are both followed by a vowel.)

/m/ harmonizes occasionally to a following consonant, as in [sɪind] *seemed* (7). This may be further subject to CCS with nasality left on the preceding vowel (see below), e.g. [sɐ̃θɪŋk̊] *something* (60). Nasalization of the preceding vowel occurs occasionally before /n/, e.g. [wɒ̃nʔtəd] *wanted* (42).

Palatal harmony is common:

[ɔːwɪʒ jɒus] *always used* (1)

[ɹɒuɪndʒə] *ruined your* (21)

[sːɹikʃ jɹiəz] *six years* (36)

[ɪʔʃ jɔːᵊ] *it's your* (38),

though there are instances where it has not applied, e.g.

[djɒu] *do you* (55).

/ð/-harmony is likewise widespread. (There are no examples of /θ/-harmony.)

[wɛɫ lɪ] *well the* (7)

[ən̩ n̪æʔs] *and that's* (15)

[ðæ̪ːʔs sə] *that's the* (23)

[æv vɪiz] *have these* (25)

[wɒn̩ʔ n̩ɪs] *want this* (24)

[kös zə] *'cos the* (44)

[bɪɫʔ lʲə] *built there* (52).

A common example of this harmony operating at a greater distance, over three segments, is [lɑɪ? læ:?] *like that* (47) and (48). We may note that /l/-vocalization must take place after /ð/-harmony, e.g.

/wɛl ðɛɪ/

/ð/-harmony   ⇒ wɛɫ lɛɪ

/l/-vocalization ⇒ [wö̜ lɛɪ] (57).

(UVD also operates on *well* in this case.) Geminate Simplification also applies in some instances after /ð/-harmony, e.g. [ɔ: læ?] *all that* (30).

One particular example, which is rather unusual, has quite a complex derivation:

/ænd ðɪi fʌɒn/

Stress placement	⇒	ənd ðə fʌ́ɒn
Place harmony	⇒	ən̪d̪ ðə fʌ́ɒn
CCS	⇒	ən̪ ðə fʌ́ɒn
/ð/-harmony	⇒	ən̪ n̪ə fʌ́ɒn
UVD	⇒	ən̪ n̪ fʌ́ɒn
Geminate simplification	⇒	[ən̪ fʌɒw̃] (45).

(Place and manner harmony have applied to the final nasal in this instance.) The fact that it is unusual is no doubt reflected by the number of processes that have operated. Furthermore, there may well be some kind of constraint on the number and/or type of rules that can' apply in any one derivation. In this case the original /n/ of *and* has not harmonized again to the following /f/, as it would do if there were no definite article, as in, for example, *and phone him*. Harmony has operated twice in this derivation; perhaps a third occurrence is ruled out.

(c) *CCS*. CCS operates, as in most accents, on /t/ and /d/:

[dʒʌs kʊdn̩ʔ] *just couldn't* (4)

[sɪim tə] *seemed to* (8)

[lʊ? sʌmθɪŋʔ] *looked something* (48)

60

[kɷŋʔ] *couldn't* (50)

[paɷnz] *pounds* (51).

The oral closure of /n/ is deleted with nasality on the preceding vowel, e.g.

[maĩz vɛɹɪi] *mine's very* (6)

[dʌɷ̃ʔ θĩʔ] *don't think* (6)

[ɒ̃ ðə] *on the* (34).

Thus, with *don't* in particular, we find either [dʌɷ̃ʔ] or a derivation with Voicing, Nasal Harmony and Geminate Simplification (see above), giving [dʌɷn], as in [dʌɷn wɒnə] *don't want to* (62). There are no examples of /n/-deletion in such words (cf. Stockport above), that is forms such as *[dʌɷʔ] do not occur (but cf. Wells, 1982: 318, who gives the form [dᶻʌʔnʌːᵘ], *don't know*, though this may be untypical).

The sequence /ng/ is always realized as [ŋ] at a morpheme boundary, as in standard English (cf. Chomsky and Halle, 1968: 85). This means a /g/-deletion rule operating on this environment after place harmony of /n/ has occurred. Alternatively, it would be possible to treat such forms in the same way as the [nd]⇒[n] forms, which also only occur at morpheme boundaries, e.g. [dʌɷn] *don't* (62), but not *[wʌnə] *wonder*. These forms involve left-to-right Voicing, left-to-right Nasal Harmony and Geminate Simplification, which could apply to words like *sing* too:

		/kɑːnt/	/sɪng/
Voicing	⇒	kɑːnd	——
Alveolar Harmony	⇒	——	sɪŋg
L-to-R N Harmony	⇒	kɑːnn	sɪŋŋ
Geminate Simplif.	⇒	[kɑːn]	[sɪŋ].

(At some stage in the history of English this process eliminated the final /b/ from words such as *lamb*.)

The present participle ending has both the /-ɪng/ and the /-ɪn/ suffix. It is perhaps significant that only the former occurs at the beginning of the conversation, whereas the latter appears also later on, e.g. [lɪvɪn] *living* (57), [mɛɪkɪn] *making* (62). This may indicate that the informant is conscious of being recorded to start with, but settles down after a few minutes. The words ending in unstressed *-thing*, e.g. *something*, have either [-ɪŋʔ] or [-ɪŋ]. The former seems to occur when the following sound has a contoid articulation, e.g.

[sʌmθɪŋ? laɪ?] (47) and (48)

[sæ̃θɪŋk̚? tə] (60) (with velar closure as well),

but [ɛnɪθɪŋ ɪf sʌmθɪŋ hæpm̃nd] (20-21).

(Wells, 1982: 317, suggests that the form underlying
something, and, presumably, all the other words ending in unstressed -*thing*, ends in /-θɪŋk/. Whilst
this may be the case for some broader London speech-
types, in C's speech the [?] with or without a
simultaneous velar closure is epenthetic rather than
underlying.)

(d) *UVD*. There are a number of examples of UVD which
are commonly found in most varieties of colloquial
spoken English, e.g.

  [lɛɪt'ɪɒn] *later on* (29)

  [sə] *It's a* (40)

  [aɷ? ðə] *out of the* (48)

  [ʃb] *should* (42).

[ən fʌɷw̃] is discussed above. [dʒö mɛmbə] *Do you
remember* (31) is also common in spoken English: the
vowel of *do*, as an unstressed auxiliary verb, is
deleted, and so is the first vowel of *remember*. In
the latter case /r/-deletion operates as well, giving
the following derivation:

                /dɷu jɷu rɪmɛmbr̩/

  Stress placement   ⇒   dɷ jɷ rɪmémbə

  UVD (x 2)   ⇒   dʒörmémbə

  /r/-deletion   ⇒   [dʒö mémbə].

(I have omitted details irrelevant to the present
discussion, e.g. Palatal Harmony.)

(e) *Linking r*. Linking r is used in most cases intervocalically, but not always, e.g.

  [p'ɛɪpəɹ a̲] *paper I* (3)

  [mɔ:ɹ ə] *more or* (4)

  [sɛɹ ʌɷ ĩ] *their own* (24)

  [heə ən] *hair and* (2).

There are no examples of "intrusive" r.

(f) *Vowel lengthening*. The open vowels /æ/ and /ɛ/
lengthen before a nasal consonant in a final stressed
syllable; /n/ may be followed by /d/, e.g.

[hæ:nd] *hand* (4)

[ɛ:nd] *end* (5)

[stæ:nd] *stand* (22)

[ʌndəstæ:mb] *understand* (39).

This applies even when the stress is secondary rather than main, e.g. [tɛlɪgɹæ:m] *telegram* (42) (and in the plural (43)). /ɛ/ does not always lengthen, e.g. [sɛn̩n̩] *send* (42), and the other vowels never do, e.g. [blɒnd] *blond* (26), [dʌn] *done* (24). Stressed *that* also tends to have a lengthened vowel phase, e.g. [ðæ:t̚] (43).

Chapter Three

PEASMARSH, SUSSEX

There are two informants, both women. Informant W,
aged 87, lived in Peasmarsh all her life; informant B,
aged 64, was born at nearby Sellindge but moved to
Peasmarsh in her teens and has lived there ever since.

(i) *General*
Both speakers have a relatively tense musculature.
The voiceless stops are only weakly aspirated initi-
ally, /t/ more than the other two. /r/ is post-
alveolar and following consonants, which are alveolar
elsewhere, have a tendency to be post-alveolar too
(see below under Harmony).
     Lip-rounding is produced without protrusion and
is most apparent in [ɔ:], [ɵ] and [ɷ]. In the other
vocoid articulations lip-position varies from spread
to neutral. Speaker B sometimes has slight lip-
rounding in the initial phase of the diphthong in
time [ɒ̹ɪ].

(ii) *Vowel diagrams*
I have put both speakers on the same diagrams, as
they are for the most part the same. B regularly has
three different articulations, which I have bracketed
on the diagrams.

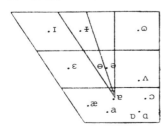

short monophthongs

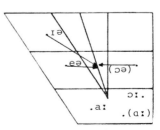

long monophthongs and
centralizing diphthongs

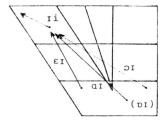
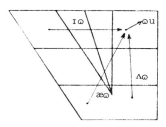

front closing
diphthongs

back closing
diphthongs

(iii) *The transcription of speaker W*

1 ˀέɪwɔɹdn̩ ǽɒs ɪˀ wəz kɔ́ːɫd | jɨ́ɹz əgʌɒ | bʌt ɑɪ θɪ́ŋg̊ ɪˀs

2 kɔ́ːɫd sʌ́mθɪŋ̊ έɫs næɒ

Hawarden House it was called / years ago / but I think
it's called something else now.

3 ðɪ ʌ́ɒɫd fǽʃnn̩ nɛɪm wəz̊ έɪwɔɹdn̩ | ðætˀ kʊ́tɹɪdʒ

The old-fashioned name was Hawarden / that cottage.

4 ʃɹi njɪ́ɒ wɛn ɪˀ wəz gɔ́ɪnə ɹέɪn | wέn ʃɹ wəz dɔ́ʊɪŋ kɔ́ɹsɪts |

5 ɐn ʃɹ jɪ́ɒstˈə lέɪ əɹ kɔ́ɹsɪts dǽɒn pɔ́d̊ əɹ ǽ·nᵈz ä̩n ðə tέɪbɫ

6 n̩ gʌ́ɒ ɔ·f tə slɪ́ip

She knew when it was going to rain / when she was doing
corsets / and she used to lay her corsets down put her
hands on the table and go off to sleep.

7 wέn ʃɹ wəz mǽɹɪd ʃɹ wəz wəɹkɪŋ fə mɪ́stəɹ fɪ́ɫməɹ | ðə

8 glʌ́vɹɪ | glʌ́vz̊ ən lέgɪnz̊ ən spǽts əz ðɛɪ jɪ́ɒstə kɔ́ːɫ ɫəm

When she was married she was working for Mister Filmer /
the glovery / Gloves and leggings and spats as they used to
call them.

9 ðɛɪ stáɹtɪd ɪm wä́ɪtnä́ɪts | ðə mɪ́dɫ ǽɒs əv ðʌ́ɒs θɹɨ́i

They started in Whiteknights / the middle house of those 3.

65

10   ʃɹi dɪdn̩ wɜ́ɹk fəɹ énibaɹɪ

       She didn't work for anybody.

11   ɐ spöꭥz ɪ? wó·z | aɪ ka·n ɹ́ivtɕ ɹɪmémbɹ ɹ dóuɪŋ əm | ʌóni

12   ðət ʃɹi dɪ́dˀdꭥu əm

       I suppose it was / I can't even remember her doing them /
       only that she did do them.

13   ɹáɪt ʌp ? ðə táp əv ðə stɹɨit˥

       Right up at the top of the street.

14   maɪ fá·ðəɹ ɪz̥ níəɹɪs ðə fɛ́nᵗs | maɪ mʌ́ðəɹ ən aɪ əɹ ət̪ ðə

15   gɛɪt

       My father is nearest the fence / My mother and I are at the
       gate.

16   ʌóni dʒʌ́st ə péɪvmɨn? nǽɹöꭥ péɪvmɨn? bɪtwíin̥ n̥ë hǽꭢs ən̥ n̥ë

17 | fɛ́ns

       Only just a pavement narrow pavement between the house and
       the fence.

18   dǽꭢn ɛgzó͡ɯɫ | bádm əv ðə hɪ́ɫ | ən θɹíi pˈɬɹ́ismən ɑ́n͡m pó̥ɪnt˥

19   díutɪ | ən maɪ vá·ðəɹ sɛd ə | ɪ? wəz əβǽꭢ? mídnaɪtˈ | sʌ́ꭢ

20   áɪ æd tˈə gʌ́ꭢ wɪ́ð ɪm ë̞ɛ́ɬp˺ pˈṍʃ ðə g̊aɹt | dʒʌ́ss ə tˈóu

21   wɹíɫd tɹʌ́k laɪk | köɹs zə kˈáfɪm wəz kʌ́vəɹd ʌ́·pˈ | əʒ jóuʒꭢ

22 | wɛ́m wɹi gát˥dǽꭢn də ðə báɹm əv égzʌɫ ?ɨ́ɫ ðɛ wəɹ θɹíi

23   pˈɬɹ́ismən ɑ́n͡m pó̥ɪnt˥díutˈɪ | ænd maɪ vá·ðəɹ sɛ́d˺tˈꭢ əm ɪts

24   ɔ́: ɹáɪ? wɹiv gḁ́d ə lǽ·ntəɹn bəd ɪts bǽk ʌp ðə ɹʌ́ꭢd

       Down Eggshole / bottom of the hill / and three policemen on
       point duty / and my father said er / it was about midnight
       / so I had to go with him er help push the cart / Just a
       two-wheeled truck, like / 'Course the coffin was covered up
       / as usual / When we got down to the bottom of Eggshole
       Hill, there were three policemen on point duty / and my
       father said to them it's all right, we've got a lantern but
       it's back up the road.

25   ?ǽd tꭢ ɪŋ n̥ə féɹs wɛ́ɹɫd wóɹ kəz ɔ́:ɫ ɪz mɛ́n wə kó:ɫd ʌ́·p |

26   ðɛn aɪ ǽd˺ tə bɪ bóɪ | gɹáɪnn̥ n̥ə wáɪ? lɛ́d nd ðə ɹɛ́d lɛ́d fə

27 ðə pɛɪn? | mɪ́ks ʌp ðə pʌ́tɪi ən sʌtʃ laɪk̚? | s·g̊ɹáɪnd ɪt ʌ́p

28 ət ðǽt̚ táɪm ə deɪ kəz ɪ? jóus? k'ʌ́m ɪn ə bɪ́g̚ k'ɛ́g | ɪ́n̩ n̩ðə

29 pɛ́ɪnt | jɷ ad̚ tə gɹáɪnd ɪd ʌ́p kəz ɪt̑p wəz láɪk:ꞌ kláɡg̚ꞌ

30 təgɛ́ðəɹ jə sɪ́i

Had to in the First World War 'cos all his men were called
up / Then I had to be boy / Grind the white lead and the
red lead for the paint / mix up the putty and such like /
Used to grind it up at that time of day 'cos it used to
come in a big keg / In the paint / you had to grind it up
'cos it was like clogged together, you see.

31 jɷu ad̚ t'ə mɪ́ks ɪt ʃəsɛ́ɫf

You had to mix it yourself.

32 ɪ́i wəz bɔ́ɹn ̩ ðɛ ɪɲ ə sɛ́ɪm ɹɷum áɪ wəz bɔ́ɹn ̩ ɪn

He was born there in the same room I was born in.

33 ðə fɛ́ɹs laɾ ə bǽʃfəɹdz lɪ́vd ɪn: | wɛ́ɹ maɪ gɹǽŋvəɹ lɪ́vv̥ |

34 ɪn̩ n̩ǽ? kɔ́ɹnɹ ǽɷs

The first lot of Bashfords lived in / where my granfer
(= grandfather) lived / in that corner house.

35 jɷ́u kt̬ ? ɹɪmɛ́mbɹ əm ðéəɹ

You can remember them there.

36 wɒ́z ɪ? ?máɪd ə bɪ́n

Was it? It might have been.

37 ðɛɪ dáɪd ɔ̥́:f

They died off.

38 ən̩ ðə ?ǽɷs wəz ̥ dʒəs lɛ́f tə ɹɷ́uɪnz ̩

And the house was just left to ruins.

39 ɫi lɪ́vd əd ə sɔ́ɹd ̩ əv ə gɛ́ɪt' | ə lɪdɫ bʌ́ŋgɫʌɷ ɔ̩ɫ an ɪz ʌ́ɷn

40 | fɪ́ɫθɹi dɛ́ɹt'ɹi ʌɷ́ɫ mǽ:n

He lived at a sort of a gate / a little bungalow all on
his own / filthy dirty old man.

41 ɪ joʊs tə weɪç f ɛnɪbɒdɪ əd ɪmp'lɔ́ɪ ɪ̨m | bət nʌ́ɒbᵊdɪ áɪdlɪ

42 wɔ́d: ɪmp'lɔ́ɪ ɪ̨m

He used to work for anybody who'd employ him / but nobody
hardly would employ him.

43 ɪtp̂ wɔ́dˀbɨi

It would be.

44 wɛ̨ᵊ maɪ sístɹɪnlɔ́: lívv ðæd ǽɒs ɪz dǽɒn tə ðə gɹǽɒn

Where my sister-in-law lived, that house is down to the
ground.

45 wɪ ad ən ɔ́ɹgənɪss fɹəm ɹáɪ | ən əɹ fɹénn | ən̨ ðén̲ ʃɪi wəz

46 t'ɒk ít̲ wɪð ə néɹvəs bɹɛ́ɪkḁǽɒn

We had an organist from Rye / and her friend / and then
she was took ill with a nervous breakdown.

47 ðə víkəɹ | wʌ́ndəɹz if jɒu kɒd ɛ́ɨp ǽɒ? wɪð ðə | féɹs láɪn

48 əv ɛ́vɹɪ ím

The vicar / wonders if you could help out with the / first
line of every hymn.

49 aɪv névəɹ tʌ́tʃt ə ɔ́ɹgən ɪn mɪ láɪf | aɪ dʌnɒ ?énɪθɪn əbæɒd

50 ən ɔ́ɹgən | ən aɪ dʌ́ɒn? θíŋk ?ǽt nʌ́ɒz énɪθɪŋ əbæɒ? míi

I've never touched a organ in my life / I don't know anything about an organ / and I don't think that knows anything about me.

51 ɹi sɛd w joʊ tɔ́:g ɪd ʌ́ɒvə wɪð ǽɹɪi wɛn ɹi kʌ́mz ɪn tə lʌ́ntʃ

He said, Well, you talk it over with Harry when he comes in
to lunch.

52 ɹi stáɹtɪd ɔ:f bǽkˀ t'ə wéɹk | əm bǽk ɹi kʌ́m | ɹi séd wɛ́t̲ |

53 pɹǽpʃ jɒudˀ gɛt θɹɔ́u ðǽ·tˀ | sʌɒ ɔ́:f ʌp ðə víkəɹz aɪ wén? | ɹi

54 wəz | ʌ́pˀ táps kəz aɪdˀgɔ́:n ʌp ? síi ɪm | ən aɪ ǽt ? gɒ ...

55 ?ɔ́t̲ θɹɒu ðɹi ímz an ə blɔ́umɪn πɹǽnʌɒ

He started off back to work / and back he come / He said,
Well / perhaps you'd get through that / So off up the
vicar's I went / He was / up tops 'cos I'd gone up to see
him / and I had to go ... all through the hymns on a
blooming piano.

68

(iv) *The transcription of speaker B*

56 ʃɪi æd ə ʃɒ́k˺ dɪ́dn̩ ʃɪ́i

She had a shock, didn't she?

57 ɪʔ jɷ́us ʔ bɪ̯ ɹɪ́ilɪ wʌ́ndəfɫ̩ dɷ́u ɹɪ́ilɪi | ənd ɛ́vɹɪwɛɹ dʒɔ́ɪnd

58 ɪ́:n | ɔ́:ɫ ðə vɪ́lɪdʒɪz̥ | jɷ́us tʻ æv ɔ́:ɫ dɹɛ́s kɑ́ɹts

It used to be really wonderful do, really / and everywhere joined in / all the villages / used to have all dressed carts.

59 wɪ jɷ́us tə gʌ́ɷ ɹǽɷn̪n̪ ðə dɪ́fɹən ǽɷzɪz̥

We used to go round the different houses.

60 wɪ́i jɷus tə bɪ sɪ́ŋɪŋ wʌ́n ɛ́nn əð̃ ðə bǽ:nn wəz̥ plɛ̯́ɪɪn̪ ðɪi

61 ʌ́ðəɹ ɛ́nd ʒɷ nʌɷ

We used to be singing one end and the band was playing the other end, you know.

62 wɪ jɷus tə stɑ́:tʼ ɔ́:f | wʌ́n ǽɷs wɷd ə ɛ́ntˈətˈɛ̯́ɪn əs |

63 wɪ jɷus t æv ɹʌ́m pʌ́ntʃ ən ... ɔ́: sɔ·ts ə lɪɫ̩ snǽks ɪn̪ ðéəɹ

We used to start off / one house would er entertain us / We used to have rum punch and ... all sorts of little snacks in there.

64 wɪ ɔ́:ɫ wɛnt ɪndɔ̣́əz əv kɔ̣́əs z̃ sǽʔ n̪ n̪ə dɹɔ́:ɪŋ ɹɷumz ən dɪ́d

65 ɛəɹ sɪ́ŋɪn | ən tɑ́ɪm wɪ gɑtʻ hʌ́ɷm wɪi wəz̥ vɛ́ɹɪ mɛ́ɹɪi jɷ nʌ́ɷ

We all went indoors, of course, and sat in the drawing rooms and did our singing / and time we got home, we was very merry, you know.

66 wɪ jɷus tə sɪ́ŋ ɔ́:ɫ lə wɛɪ hʌ́ɷm bət nɑ́ʔ kǽɹəɫz

We used to sing all the way home, but not carols.

67 wɪ jɷus t ǽv mʌ́ɷst ɪndʒɔ́ɪəbö tɒ̣ɪm

We used to have (a) most enjoyable time.

68 wɒ́n̩t ʃɷu ɪn̪ n̪ə tʻɪ́im

Wasn't you in the team?

69 ðæts ɔ:° dʉ́ɪd ǽʊt náʊ
   That's all died out now.

70 lʌ́ndənəɹz̥ bʉ́ɪ ə ... ǽv və kádɪdʒɪz̥ fə wɪ́ikénd
   Londoners buy er ... have the cottages for (a) week-end.

71 ðɛn̥ n̥æ? mɪ́inz̥ zə pɪ́ipɬ ɵuv | gád ə gʌ́ʊ ɪntə ðə kǽʊnsɬ áʊzɪz̥
   Then that means the people who've (?) / got to go into the
   council houses.

72 sɛ́vəm pǽʊŋψ fəɹ s̲ɹɪ́i bɛ́dɹʊum
   Seven pound for three bedroom ...

73 ðɛ̈ vɛ́ɹii náɪs | kəs zəz̥ ná? mɛnɹi váɹm kátɪdʒɪz̥ nǽʊ ɪz zə
   They're very nice. / 'Course there's not many farm cottages
   now, is there?

74 kəs zʌ́ʊz̥ kátɪdʒɪz̥ dǽʊn̥ ðə bʉ́dəm ðɛ̯əɹ wɒ? wə́:ɹ váɹm kátɪdʒʃ
75 bɪn sʌ́ʊɬd ǽvn̥ n̥ɛ́ɪ
   'Course those cottages down the bottom there what were farm
   cottages (have) been sold, haven't they?

76 ðɛɪ tʉ́? ðə θǽtʃ áv̥ əm pʉ́? ðə slɛ́ɪt' ɑn dɪ́dn̥ ðɛɪ
   They took the thatch off and put the slate on, didn't they?

77 ɪf jʊ gʏ́ʊ tə sɪ́i əɹ hə́:ɹ hǽÿs ɪz ən ʌ́ʊɬd θǽtʃt háʊs
   If you go to see her, her house is an old thatched house.

78 ʃɪ jʉ́ust˺ tə lɪ́v ət ðə táp ə ðə stɹɪ́it
   She used to live at the top of the street.

79 skʉ́ʊɬ lɛ́ɪn wəz dɹɛ́dfö wɛw̃ wɪ wɛ́nt | ? wz ɔ́:° pʉ́thʌʊ:z | ɪ̣?
80 wz ʌ́ʊnlɪ wɛn̥ n̥ə wɔ́: kɛ́ɪm ðə? ðɛɪ mɛ́ɪd ðə ɹʌ́ʊd ʌp
   School Lane was dreadful when we went. / It was all pot-
   holes. / It was only when the war came that they made the
   road up.

81 ðɛ́n ðɛɪ dɪsʉ́ɪdɪd tə mɛ́ɪk ðə ɹʌ́ʊd ʌp wɪ ðɪ á:ᛁmɹi
   Then they decided to make the road up with the Army.

82 kɔs wɪ jɑ́us t æv ə fɔ́ɹdʒ íəɹ ə gɑ́d mɛnɪ jíəɹz ən nǽɷ ɪˀs

83 klʌ́ɷz dá·ɷn | wɪtʃ wəz ɹá:ɹeɷ ə ʃǽ·ɪm aɪ θíːŋk

'Course we used to have a forge here a good many years and
now it's closed down / which was rather a shame, I think.

84 ðɹi ə súɪkɫ ʃúp jɷus ə βɪ aṇ ṇɪ ʌ́ðə saɪd ðə ɹéɷd

The er cycle shop used to be on the other side (of) the
road.

85 və̀ɹɪ ʌɷɫd mɪ́stə vá:ɹlë lív ðëɹ | ðə vá:ðəɹ əv ɔ́: ðʌɷz

Very old Mr Farley lived there / the father of all those.

86 ạ̈ ʃt θíŋk sʌɷ jë́:

I should think so, yes.

87 ðə wəz ʌ́ɷnlɪ bʌ́s wɛnˀ twä̈ɪs ə wɹ́ik

There was   only (a) bus went twice a week.

88 wɛ́nzdɪ̣ má:ɹkɪtˀdéɪ ǽnd án: ə sǽtədɛɹ

Wednesday market day and on er Saturday.

89 ðɛɪ wz wʌ́ndəfö | bət ɪf ðə dɹʊ́ɪvəɹ wʊ́nɪd ? pɒp ín n æv ɪẓ

90 tˀíi jö jɷus tˀæv də wɛ́ɪˀ fə hím jɷ síi

They was wonderful / But if the driver wanted to pop in
and have his tea, you used to have to wait for him, you
see.

91 a:ftə ð̥ fə́ɹṣ wə́ɹḻ wó:ᵊɹ | ᵊwəz nʌ́ɷ tɹá:z̃spɔ·ˀ wɒˀsʌɷévʌ

After the First World War / there was no transport what-
soever.

92 i maɪd ə gad ə báɪk sáɪkɫ

You might have got a bike, cycle.

93 ɪˀ wəz ə və́ɹɪi pó:ɹ ʌɷɫ plɛ̣́ɪs wɛw̃ wɹi fə́ɹṣ kɛ̣́ɪm híʌ

It was a very poor old place when we first came here.

94 ðə wəz nʌ́ɷ wó:təɹ ïṇ ṇæˀ hǽɷs ä̈ɹ ɛ́nɪθɪŋ | wɪ ǽdˀ də fʊ́ɪnd ə

95 spɹíŋ ǽɷtˀ ɪṇ ðə wɷ́dˀdə gɛd ɛɷ wó:tˢəᴵ

There was no water in that house or anything / We had to
find a spring out in the wood to get our water.

96 ɔ:ɫ ɛəɹ klʌ́b mémbəz

All our club members.

97 wʊ́ʒ jɒu ðéəɹ

Was you there?

98 äv dʌ́n sʌm θíɳz ɪm mɪ tpɪm | äv lɒ́kt á:ftəɹ ə pǽɹət͈ʼ

I've done some things in my time / I've looked after a
parrot.

99 ən ɪ? wʊ́zn̩ ɪn ə kɛ́ɪdʒ

And it wasn't in a cage.

100 ɪf ə jɒu wʊ́·ntɪd͈ʼ də gɛ́d ɪd ɔ́·f ðe flɔ́:ə̇ɹ ... jɒu ǽd ə pɒt͈ʼ

101 də kɛ́ɪdʒ dǽɒn fɔɹ ɪt͈ʼ də klɑ́ɪm ɑn

If you wanted to get it off the floor ... you had to put
the cage down for it to climb on.

(v) *Phonological discussion*
Both speakers have the /ɒ/-/-/ʌ/ distinction, sporadic
use of /h/, unstressed word-final /ɪi/ (though not
in all instances), and syllable-final /r/, though
there are instances of its disappearance in B's
speech (see below). [ŋ] occurs without a following
[g].

(a) *Lenition.* The voiceless stops and fricatives,
which are otherwise fortis, are given lenis articulations, either voiced or voiceless, usually between
voiced sounds, e.g.

[mɑɪd ə] *might have* (36) and (92)

[mɑɪ va·ðəɹ] *my father* (19)

[tɔ:g ɪd ʌɒvə] *talk it over* (51)

[ǽd də] *had to* (94).

Although there are certain common occurrences of
lenition, as in *got to* and *had to*, it does not always
occur: for example, B says [kɑdɪdʒɪz] for *cottages*
(70), but also says it twice, (73) ånd (74), with [t].
In the case of /t/, speaker W sometimes uses a flap,
as in [lɑɾ ə] *lot of* (33). Speaker B has one instance of lenition after a voiceless sound: [ɪt də] *it*

72

to (101).

On one occasion each speaker applies lenition to /b/ intervocalically producing a fricative:

[əβæɒʔ] *about* (19)

[ə βɪ] *to be* (84).

This appears to be a sporadic feature of rapid speech. Speaker B deletes /t/ in a few instances:

[lɪɫ] *little* (63)

[jɒus ə] *used to* (84)

[æd ə] *had to* (100).

From the data in the recordings it is difficult to see what the derivation of these forms might be (other than an *ad hoc* /t/-deletion rule, which is unsatisfactory, if some other rule(s) can be invoked), though they occur in rapid articulations and are not the same as the major processes under consideration in this book. It is just possible that Geminate Simplification can be triggered by matching place features only in B's system rather than by a matched set of features: thus, in each case above we have two segments with alveolar contact, one of which is deleted. In each case it is the underlying /t/ that is deleted regardless of the order of the two seg-ments. If such an explanation is justified, then we are dealing with an adaptation of an existing rule to remove the /t/.

/l/ is frequently vocalized and sometimes dele-ted in post-vocalic and post-consonantal syllabic positions:

[jɒuʒɒ] *usual* (21)

[ɔ: ɹaɪʔ] *all right* (24)

[ɔ:] *all* (63) and (85)

[dɹɛdfö] *dreadful* (79)

[pɒthʌɒ:z] *pot-holes* (79).

One interesting lenition feature is /r/-deletion. In post-vocalic position we find a number of slightly different articulations which plot stages in the disappearance of /r/; for example:

[jɪəɹ̥z̥] (82) retracted frictionless continuant
            with retracted following consonant

[mɛmbəz̲] (96) retracted consonant only

[ɑ:ᶧmɪi] (81) slight continuant

[kɔ̣əs] (64) vocalization with non-retracted consonant

[hɪʌ] (93) altered vowel quality

[stɑ:t] (62))
[ʌðə] (84)) deletion.
[ɛɷ] (95))

All the above examples are from B; speaker W only has three instances and these are in unstressed syllables:

[ʃəsɛɫf] (31)

[wɛ̣^{ə}] (44)

[ʌɷvə] (51).

Despite its deletion by B, both speakers have an underlying /r/ in post-vocalic position. In younger speakers, however, there is evidence to suggest that in some cases it has disappeared, the accent of these speakers being non-rhotic.

(b) *Devoicing*. The feature of final devoicing of voiced stops and fricatives in prepausal position and before voiceless sounds, which is widespread in most accents of English, occurs in the speech of both speakers even before voiced sounds, in word-final position and after /s/. All the examples in B's speech are of the verbal and plural s-endings. For example:

[wɵz̥] *was* (1), (3) and (4)

[kɔ:ɫd̥] *called* (2)

[bæʃfəɹd̥z̥] *Bashfords* (33)

[z̥ə] *the* (21)

[g̊ɹɑɪnd] *grind* (27)

[wəz̥] *was* (60) and (83)

[z̥əz̥] *there's* (73).

It is interesting to note that this goes in the opposite direction, as it were, from lenition, which is widespread in these speakers. It also appears to be restricted to the s-endings in B's speech in comparison to W's.

(c) *Harmony*. The alveolars /t d n/ display place harmony with a following consonant:

[kˈɑfɪm wɵz] *coffin was* (21)

[ət̪ ðə] *at the* (14)

[gɹæŋvəɹ] *grandfather* (33)

[sɛvəm pæoŋ̩ψ fəɹ] *seven pound for* (72).

Sometimes the alveolar and the following place articulation are virtually simultaneous in W's speech, e.g.

[ɑn͡m pǫɪnt] *on point* (18) and (23)

[ɪt͡p wɛz] *it was* (29).

A syllabic /n/ will in some cases harmonize with the preceding consonant:

[ɹivn̩] *even* (11)

[kn̩] *can* (35).

Place and manner harmony occur occasionally: [wɛw̃ wɪ] (79) and (93).
Since /r/ is a post-alveolar frictionless continuant, it produces harmony in following alveolar consonants, e.g.

[bɔɹn] *born* (32)

[kɔɹnɹ] *corner* (34)

[deɹt'ɹi] *dirty* (40)

[fəɹs weɹl] *First World* (91).

This harmony does not always occur, e.g.

[staɹtɪd] *started* (52)

[kɑɹts] *carts* (58).

/r/ also appears to have an influence on adjacent front vowels, making them more centralized, e.g.

[jɨɹz] *years* (1)

[θɹɨi] *three* (9)

[vɛ̈ɹɪ] *very* (65).

This, too, does not always take place, e.g. [θɹɪi] (18) and (22). In B's speech the commonest word to show /r/-vowel harmony is *very*, which regularly has [ə] as its first vowel, even when it is stressed, as in lines (85) and (93).

The left-to-right nasal harmony displayed by informant C in the previous chapter is found in both speakers here, with and without Geminate Simplification. For example:

[fæʃnn] *fashioned* (3)

[gɹɑɪnn̩] *grind* (26)

[gɹæɐn] *ground* (44)

[fɹɛnn] *friend* (45)

[ka·n] *can't* (11)

[ɹæɐn̩n̩] *round* (59)

[ɛnn] *end* (60)

[bæːnn] *band* (60)

[dɪfɹən] *different* (59)

[wɒnɪd] *wanted* (89)

[wɒzn̩] *wasn't* (99).

There are exceptions to this process, e.g. [g̊ɹɑɪnd] (27), [ɛnd] (61). In B's speech it would appear from the data that /nt/ reduces to [n] but /nd/ does not, which suggests a different state of affairs from the one discussed in the previous chapter, where both reduce. In B's case /nd/ has the left-to-right harmony, whereas /nt/ does not. The latter seems to be another instance of the modified GS rule mentioned above, which removes a /t/ adjacent to any other alveolar consonant. In W's case the resultant [nn] from /nd/ is simplified by GS occasionally; /nt/ is subject to the modified GS rule, as in B's speech. The difference between these two informants and informant C is that there are no instances here of /nt/→[nd] (cf. previous chapter).

In W's speech in some instances /d/ and /t/ are subject to this left-to-right harmony, e.g.

[dʒʌss] *just* (20)

[klɑgg] *clogged* (29)

[lɪvv̥] *lived* (33) and (44, without devoicing)

[ɔɹgənɪss] *organist* (45).

We can see from the above that it involves both place and manner harmony.

ð-harmony, which involves both left-to-right harmony and manner harmony, is common in both speakers, e.g.

[kɔːɫ ɫəm] *call them* (8)

[köɹs z̥ə] *course the* (21)

[ɪn̩ n̩ə] *in the* (25)

[gɹɑɪnn n̩ə] *grind the* (26)

[θɪŋk ʔæt̚] *think that* (50)

[ɔːɫ lə] *all the* (66)

[æv və] *have the* (70)
[kəs zəz] *course there's* (73)
[wɛɳ ɳə] *when the* (80)
[pɒt də] *put the* (100-01).
θ-harmony has only one instance:
[fəɹ s̠ɹii] *for three* (72).
This is caused by the surrounding [r]-articulations
and is not the same as in the instances discussed in
Lodge (1981: 29).
    In B's speech manner harmony applies to /n/
occasionally, e.g.
[əð̃ ðə] *and the* (60)
[z̃ sæʔ] *and sat* (64)
[tɹɑːz̃spɔ·ʔ] *transport* (91).
W has only one example of manner harmony which is
probably just a sporadic occurrence: [wəɹç f] (41).
Voice harmony, which is not very widespread in
English accents, (cf. Introduction, p. 9), appears
in B's speech in [ʃt θɪŋk̊] *should think* (86) and
probably in [ð fəɹs̠] *the first* (91).
    Finally, °we find palatal harmony in both speak-
ers, e.g.
[əʒ jouʒɷ] *as usual* (21)
[ɪt ʃəsɛɫf] *it yourself* (31)
[pɹæpʃ joudˀ] *perhaps you'd* (41)
[ɛnd ʒɷ] *end you* (48)
[wɒnt ʃou] *wasn't you* (56)
[wɒʒ jou] *was you* (85).
(d) *CCS*. CCS applies to /t/ and /d/:
[nɪəɹɪs ðə] *nearest the* (14)
[dʒəs lɛf tə] *just left to* (38)
[ʌɷɫ mæːn] *old man* (40)
[dɹɛs kɑɹts] *dressed carts* (58)
[klʌɷz da·ɷn] *closed down* (83)
[lɪv ðëɹ] *lived there* (85)
[fəɹs̠ wəɹɫ wɔːᵊɹ] *First World War* (91).
There are no examples where /n/ is deleted in /-nt/
sequences; it would appear not to apply to these two

speakers. [ŋ] can be treated as /ng/, as in
Shepherd's Bush; there are the usual two forms of the
present participle, in [-ɪŋ] and [-ɪn], the latter
subject to harmony in the appropriate contexts. The
difference can be accounted for in the order of
application of the rules, e.g.

/-ɪng w-/

Alveolar harmony   ⇒   -ɪŋg w-

/g/-deletion   ⇒   -ɪŋ w-

as in [sɪŋɪŋ wʌn] (60);

/-ɪng ð-/

/g/-deletion   ⇒   -ɪn ð-

Alveolar harmony   ⇒   -ɪn̯ ð-

as in [plɛɪɪn̯ ðɪi] (60).

(e) *UVD*. In B's speech, when there are two unstressed
vowels together and one of them is [ə], the [ə] is
deleted, e.g.

[jɑus tæv] *used to have* (58),(63), (67) and (82)

[ʌɑnlɪ bʌs] *only a bus* (87).

She also deletes [ə] following /w/, as in [wz] *was*
(79), (80) and (89) (cf. Stockport above). In phonetic terms both [w] and [ə] are vocoid articulations
and in rapid speech can easily be run together. The
tongue position for the resultant articulation is
roughly that of [ö], the lip-rounding being retained,
but it is not a syllable nucleus, so that it can be
suitably transcribed as [w]. (Where there is a preceding [ʔ], as at (79) and (80), that, too, has lip-
rounding.)

[f ɛnɪbɒdɪ] (41) is W's only example of [ə]-
deletion before a vowel, and here it is only possible
because of a previous /r/-deletion. This may also be
an explanation of B's [fə wɪikɛnd] (70).

The most common deletion of [ə] is following [ʔ];
this occurs in both speakers, e.g.

[ʌp ʔ sɪi] *up to see* (54)

[æt ʔ gɑ] *had to go* (54)

[jɑus ʔ. bɪ] *used to be* (57)

[wɒnɪd ʔ pɒp] *wanted to pop* (89).

In one instance the [ə] precedes [ʔ]: [ʌp ʔ] *up at*
(13).

78

(f) *Vowel lengthening.* Vowels in stressed syllables in lento speech are lengthened in most English accents, and there are some examples of this in the data under consideration here, e.g. [ʌ·p] (21) and (25), [θɪːŋk] (83), [da·ɒn] (83), [ʃæ·ɪm] (83). On the other hand, there is lengthening of low vowels before /n/, as in [læ·ntəɹn] (24), [gɔːn] (54), [bæːnn] (60). The lengthened vowel before voiceless fricatives, as in RP *father, class* and so on, is still apparent in *off* (6), (37), (52), (53), (62) and (100).

Chapter Four

EDINBURGH

There are two male informants: G, aged 50, who was
born in Harburn, about 16 miles from Edinburgh, and
moved to the city to start work, and H, aged 19, who
was born and educated in Edinburgh, but moved out to
Penicuik at the age of 5. As a child, G used a broad
Scots dialect (cf. Wells, 1982: 393-99) quite different from his present accent. (I have added an
excerpt from a poem, which he recited for me in his
childhood dialect, at the end of his conversational
transcription, but I shall not be concerned with it
in the phonological discussion.)

(i) *General*
Both speakers use a relatively tense tongue in their
articulations; as a consequence there is very little
affrication of stops and the voiceless ones are not
often aspirated. The apical contact, except for /θ/
and /ð/, which are dental, is normally post-alveolar.
The vowel articulations have a tendency to be fairly
centralized, even in stressed syllables. /l/ has
either a central or back vowel colouring in all
positions (cf. Wells, 1982: 411). /r/ has a wide
range of articulations: trill, flap and frictionless
continuant. It is usually apico-post-alveolar and,
in certain contexts, voiceless. It is occasionally
retroflex: in line (85) speaker H uses considerable
retroflexion, giving an Ulster quality to that stretch
of speech. It should also be noted that where I have
written [ɾ] before another post-alveolar sound with a
complete oral closure on the median line: [t d n l],
we are not always dealing with a flap, since there
may be no on-off movement of the tongue. In such
cases we have a very short [d]-articulation. Such
pairs as *curl* and *cuddle* may, in fact, be pronounced
the same (though the latter may also undergo /l/-
vocalization).

Lip-rounding is normally produced with protrusion; [ɒ] is sometimes produced without lip-rounding, i.e. [ɑ]. Both [e] and [ɛ] are used where other accents have a short /e/ sound, e.g. G's [edɪnbɾʌh] and H's [ɛdɨnbʌɾʌh]. The close variety is the same as the equivalent of what is a diphthong in many other accents, e.g. [eti] *eighty*. Most of the vowels are found in unstressed as well as stressed syllables. Speaker G has a range of [u] to [ü] realizations for /u/, the former more common, except after /j/. [ɑ] both long and short is used by G in certain instances where RP has /ɑ/. (See also Wells' comments, 1982: 403.)

Final stops are often released, even before another stop consonant; wherever the stop symbol is left without a diacritic, that stop is released, albeit weakly.

(ii) *Vowel diagrams*

Speaker G:

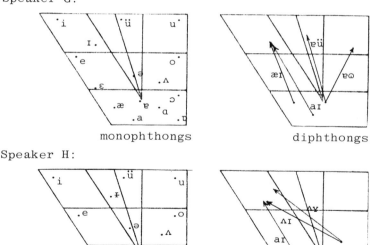

monophthongs   diphthongs

Speaker H:

monophthongs   diphthongs

[u] is not common in H's speech, occurring only in [ɛkskl̩uzɨv] (64); the front closing diphthong is sometimes °[æɪ].

(iii) *The transcription of speaker G*

1 nɔ́ʔ néωədez | no no onłë ðǽt wəz ðə wé wë spók ət hóm |

2 nʊ́t əʔ skúö | ʔ wəz wíð ðǽt ǽksēnt ɪf jë hɐd spókən ɪn énë

3 ʌðəɾ ǽksɛnt əz ə tʃɛ́ωd | jëd əv bin łáːft ɐɒt əv kóət | əz

4 p'üt'ɪ̊ŋ ɔn éɪz ən gɾésëz

Not nowadays / No no only that was the way we spoke at home
/ not at school. / It was with that accent, if you had
spoken in any other accent as a child / you'd have been
laughed out of court / as putting on airs and graces.

5 ðaʔ wəz wést˺ kɔ́łdəɾ ëʔ wz áktʃełë ʔɐ́ütseɪd wést kɔ́łdəɾ ə

6 háːmłët kɔłd háːrbʌɾn | féməs néωədez fɪ ə gɔ́łf kóɾs

That was West Calder, it was actually outside West Calder,
a hamlet called Harburn / famous nowadays for a golf course.

7 eː síkst'ɪ̈n ɔ t'ɐe twéntë mǽɪłz

Eh sixteen or to twenty miles.

8 o jés ɪndíd | a dón? no kwǽɪt'ᶜ | ʍéðəɾ wɪð ðë ínɾodz əv |

9 háɪəɾ ɛdʒükéʃn n ʍɔ́tnɔt ɪts méd enë dífɪəns | bət̥ ðəz stíł

10 kwaɪt ə səbstáːnʃəö əméωnt əv e | ðáːt áːksɛnt əɾéωnd

Oh yes indeed / I don't know quite / whether with the in-
roads of / higher education and whatnot it's made any
difference / but there's still quite a substantial amount
of that accent around.

11 ət skúö | o ɪf énëθɪŋ mebi ət skú wë spók słǽɪʔłë póʃʌ ðən

12 wʌn téndz të dü əz wʌ́n gɛts ódəɾ

At school / oh if anything maybe at school we spoke
slightly posher than one tends to do as one gets older.

13 o ðəɪ ə sévɾəł | eʔ ɪ́éndʒëz fɪəm ðə véɾë hǽɪłë ɐféktëd

14 mɔ́ɪnɪŋsǽɪd˺ tü əv koɾθ ðə nó tɾés ɑv áfɛktéʃn ət ɔ́ö ɪn̥ ðə

15 püəɪ héωzɪŋ skímz

Oh, there are several / It ranges from the very highly
affected Morningside to, of course, the no trace of affectation at all in the poor housing schemes.

16 kwæɪt ə fjüː ənd e sʌ́m ɪáːpɪdłeʰ | get ə véɾë báːd

17 ɹɛpjüteʃn fá·ɾ em | ə ɾʌf tǽɪp ténənts | nóbdë éɫs ɫ gó

18 ðéəˣ so ðë | ët éndz ʌpˈ wɪð ʔɛ́·vəbəe biŋ əv ðə sem tǽɪp

19 mɔɹ ə lés

Quite a few and some rapidly / get a very bad reputation
for um / er rough type tenants / nobody else'll go there
so they / it ends up with everybody being of the same type
more or less.

20 wʌn wüd ɔ́:ɫwez ɹéçəgnǽɪz ə glá:zgo áksɛnt jés

One would always recognize a Glasgow accent, yes.

21 spókən | ʌp tü ðə tǽɪm əf: | kíŋ dʒémz ðə ë síksθ ən fʌ́:st

22 | ʍen hí went̚ dë̥ün tü íŋgɫənd hi íntɹədjüst ə ɫát əv |

23 íŋgɫəʃ káɾɪktəɾístɪks | ɛm nót ən ékspɛɾt əɲ n̥ǽt̚ bət̪ ðǽts

24 mǽɪ ʌndəɾstándɪŋ əv ɪt

Spoken / up to the time of King James the eh sixth and
first. / When he went down to England, he introduced a lot
of / English characteristics / I'm not an expert on that,
but that's my understanding of it.

25 ɐ hád ə ɾʌ́stɪk ʌpbɾɪŋɪŋ | ɐ wózn? bɾɔt ʌ́p ət hóm jü si

I had a rustic upbringing / I wasn't brought up at home,
you see.

26 dɪdn? wʌ́ɾk ɑn ə fáɾm bʌt e ɫívd ɪn ʍót wəz̥ ə fómʌɾ

27 fáɹmhé̥üs

Didn't work on a farm but eh lived in what was a former
farmhouse.

28 nɔt̪ ðət ɐm əwéɾ ɔv nó | wéɫ ɪnɫá·nd

Not that I'm aware of, no. / Well inland.

29 am ə sívɫ séɹvənt ənd | am kɔnséɹnd wɪð ðe | ðj

30 ɐdmínɪstɹéʃn əv̥ ǽgɾɪkʌ́ɫtʃəɾəɫ ɫédʒɪsɫéʃn

I'm a civil servant and / I'm concerned with the / the
administration of agricultural legislation.

31 ðəɹ̥ ɪz̥ ɫé·s dʒʌ́stɪfɪkéʃn | ə má·hkədɫɪ dífɹənt ɫǽɪn

There is less justification / A markedly different line.

32 æɪ hæf tə gó tu ɫʌndən | pɹínsɪpəlɪ tü kɔnféˑɹ wɪð kóɫɪgz̥

33 ɪn ɫʌndən | óɹ̥ tú e ətʰénd əpón mæɪ mínɪstəɹ ɪf ðəz̥ ə

34 pɑ́ɫɪmént'ɹɪ dɪbét

I have to go to London / principally to confer with
colleagues in London / or to eh attend upon my minister,
if there's a parliamentary debate.

35 ðe ó:ɫwɪz̥ kʌm ʌ́p əɫ̥ ðə wikéˑnd

They always come up at the week-end.

36 só ə tɑ́ɹo pák ɪn̥ ðëɹ wíndo ən hɛd névʌ sín wʌn bɪfóɹ

Saw a tarot pack in their window and had never seen one
before.

37 næɪntin éti wɪɫ bí mæɪ ɹɪtǽɪɹmənt déked

1980 will be my retirement decade.

38 kípɪŋ kédʒ bʌ́ɹdz̥ | kédʒ bʌ́dz̥ əv óɫ tǽɪps

Keeping cage birds / cage birds of all types.

39 ði ónɫi bɹídɪŋ ðətʰ tük plés wəz̥ pjüɹɫɪ bæɪ ǽksɪdənt

The only breeding that took place was purely by accident.

40 ən éˑg fɹəm ən ɑ́:fɹɪkən síɫvəɹ bíɫ | ðe hɛd ɫóˑts əv ʃóts

41 bɫ ónɫɪ wʌ́n səksés | ðə bʌ́dz̥ v veɹɪ ʃóˑtʰ tǽɪf ɪt səɹvǽɪvd

42 ɪts péɹənts baɪ ónɫɪ ə véɹɪ veɹ ʃóˀə tʰ tǽɪm

An egg from an African silverbill. / They had lots of shots
but only one success / The birds have a very short life, it
survived its parents by only a very very short time.

43 ǽɪ wüd əv̥ θót ʌnjüʒɫ̩

I would have thought unusual.

44 ɔɫðo ɛv hɑ́d̥ ðɪ óˑd | bʌ́ɹd ɪn témpɹəɹɫe jü no ɪf ɪt wʌɹ̥ ʔíɫ

45 əɹ̥ sʌ́mθɪŋ əɹ índʒʌɹd̥

Although I've had the odd / bird in temporarily, you know,
if it were ill or something or injured.

46 ə pídʒən | ə wəz̥ ə stɑ́ɹtɪŋ əz̥ wéɫ

84

A pidgeon / There was a starling as well.

47 ənɬéˑs sʌ́mbədɪ wɔ́nts ðəm ən téks səm wɪðɪn ə féɾɬɪ ʃɔ́ˑtʼ

48 tǽɪm | ðe pút ðəm dé̥ω̥n ɐ θɪ́ŋk | koz ʌ́ðəwaɪz ðe wüd gét fáɪ̥

49 tü bɪ́g ə nʌ́mbʌ

Unless somebody wants them and takes them within a fairly
short time / they put them down, I think / 'cos otherwise
they would get far too big a number.

50 be̥ωt nǽɪntin fɔ́ɪ̥tɪ nǽɪn

About 1949.

51 ɔ́nɬɪ kém tü édɪnbɾʌʰ | tü stáɾ̥t wʌ́ɾkˤ

Only came to Edinburgh / to start work.

52 pɾǽɪvɪt skúːz mʌ́ɪtʃənt kʌ́mpənɪ skúːz

Private schools, merchant company schools.

53 wʌn dʌ́znt sɪ́i enɪ máˑkt pɾɔ́gɾes fɾəm ðə ɹɪzʌ́ɬts

One doesn't see any marked progress from the results.

Appendix
Three stanzas of a poem in G's Scots dialect:

ə gɾétˤmʌkɬ bótˤje mʌn bɪ̵ɬd	A great muckle boat ye mun build,
ən ɑɾkˤðə̥t kən flótˤhíç ən dɾáˑɪ	An ark that can float heich an' dry,
wɪ̵ rúm ɪntˤfəɾ ɔ́ jʌɾ en fóktˤ	Wi' room in't for a' yer ain folk
ən háˑntoɬ o káˑtoɬ fɔrbáˑɪ	An' (a) hantle o' cattle forby.
so nóaˑ roxt háɾd̥ ə̥t ðə dʒɔ́p	So Noah wrocht hard at the job,
ən séɾtʃt të ðë ʔéɾθs fáɾð̵sp bóɾdʌɾz	An' searched to the Earth's farthest borders,
ən géðəɾd̥ ðə bɪ́sts ɐn̩ ðə bʌ́ɾdz	An' gethered the beasts an' the birds,
ən téɬd̬ ðəm tü stáˑn baɪ fəɾ ɔ́ɾdʌɾz	An' telled them to stand by for orders.

ɔ ðɨ́s wʌzne dɨ́n ɔn̩ ðə kwét'   A' this wasna done on the
                                  quate,

ən níbʌɾz̥ wüd ʍaɪɫ̩z gɛðəɾ rún   An' neebours would whiles
                                  gether roun';

ðɛn nóa wüd drʌ́p ðəm ə hɨ́nt   Then Noah would drap them a
                                  hint

laɪk'ðə wé̦ðəɾ ɨz̥ gón tə brek   Like: "The weather is gaun to
   dún   break doun".

(iv) *The transcription of speaker H*

54 ðəɾ ɨz ə çjü̇·dʒ kómpleks ë ʃópɨn séntʌɾ | ɨ?s bin ɔɫ bɨ́ɫ?
55 ʌ́p ɨn̩ n̩ə sén?ʌɾ ə ðə sɨ́?ɨ | dʒʌst ɹɨ́sənt̩ɫɨ | méni pí̇ɸö
56 dón? ɫʌ́ɪk ɨ?

    There is a huge complex eh shopping centre / it's been all
    built up in the centre of the city / just recently. / Many
    people don't like it.

57 ən ɨ? wəz ðɨ óɫd ë ?ístʌɾn skɔ́?ɨʃ bʌ́s stéʃn̩ | ən̩ n̩á? wəz
58 ɔ́·ɫ ribɨ́ɫ?

    And it was the old Eastern Scottish bus station / and that
    was all rebuilt.

59 ɐ ɫɨ́v əbʌ́ẏ? θɾí maɪɫz ʌ̈ẏ?sʌɪd̩ ðə sɨ́?ɨ ɑn̩ ðə sʌ̈ẏ̇θ saɪd | ɑn̩
60 ðə ɾód tə píbɫz pénɨk'ük' | ɨ?s ə | kʌ̈ẏnsɫ hʌ̈ẏzɨn ɨsté?

    I live about three miles outside the city on the south side
    / on the road to Peebles, Penicuik. / It's a / council
    housing estate.

61 əpʌ́ɹ?ˌfəm ðə fʌ́ɹs θɾi mʌ́n̩θs

    Apart from the first three months.

62 ʌ́·v bɨn gón fɹəm ðə tʌ́ẏn ðʌ́? ɫén̩θ ə tʌ́ɪm

    I've been gone from the town that length of time.

63 ɨ́nsáed̩ ðə sɨ́?ɨ

    Inside the city.

64 ɔɫ ðə ɾíɫɨ | ɛkskɫúzɨv hʌ̈ẏzɨz | ðə ɾéts əɾ tü háɪ | fəɾ ə·
65 píp̩ɫ tə ʌ́?tʃəɫɨ ɫɨ́v̥ ðéɾ̩ | so ðeɾ nʌ́ɷ tʌ́ɹn̩n ɨnte ófɨsɨz̥ |

86

66 ɫɒ̃ʔs əv bɪ́znɪsɪz tʃɑ́ɹʔəd əkʎ̈́nʔənts | tɹávɫ bɪ́znɪsɪz

All the really / exclusive houses / the rates are too high
/ for er people to actually live there / so they're now
turning into offices / lots of businesses, chartered
accountants / travel businesses.

67 ɐ wʌ́ɹk ən̩ d̥ë kʎ̈́nte bʌ́sɪz | ʔɪkwɪ́vəɫən? ə kʎ̈ɒnʔe bʌ́sɪz
68 hiəɪ | əz fɑ́ɪ əz gáɫəʃíɫz ə gɫásgo ən noɹθ əz fɑ́ɪ əz pɛɹθ |
69 ɐ wʌ́ɹk ün̩ ðɛm | wɪð ðá·ʔ kʎ́mpne dʒü̈ən ðəh | vekéʃn | ən a
70 kən dʒə́st dɪtékt θɹü gon̩ | fáɪv mʎɪɫz ʎ̈ɒʔsʎɪd̥ d̥ə sɪ́ʔɪ tɒ̊e ə
71 pɫés kóɫb mʌ́sɫbʌɹʌʰ | ðe ə ʔáksɛnts ɹíɫe dɪ́fɹən?

I work on the county buses / equivalent of county buses
here / as far as Galashiels or Glasgow and north as far as
Perth. / I work on them / with that company during the /
vacation / and I can just detect through going / five miles
outside the city to a place called Musselburgh / the er
accent's really different.

72 pɸɛn ɐ wəz jʎ́ŋ | ɐ mǘvd ʎ̈ÿʔsʎɪd̥ d̥ə sɪ́ʔɪ | bʎʔ mʌ sɪ́stəɹz |
73 ðɛɹ ɔɫ óɫdɐ ðən me | wɛnt˺ tə skǘɫ mɛ́ɹ ɐ wəz bɒ́ən | so
74 ɪnstéd əv gon të ðə ɫók̚ɪ skǘɫ mɛ ðə nǘ hʎ̈ÿzɪn ɪsté? wɒz |
75 wi tɹávɫd ɪ́n ɛvɹɪ dé tə ðɪ́s skǘɫ | mɛɹ m ðə ɹést əv mɐ
76 fá·mɫe hɐd gón | mʌ bɹʎðð ən ʎɪ | fɛn ɐ léft pɹáɪməɹe skǘɫ
77 ɐ wɛnt tə̩ | ʔskǘɫ kóɫd sɪn? á·nθənɪz | kwʎɪʔ nɪə ðə dóks

When I was young / I moved outside the city / but my
sisters / they're all older than me / went to school where
I was born / so instead of going to the local school where
the new housing estate was / we travelled in every day to
this school / where um the rest of my family had gone / my
brother and I. / When I left primary school I went to /
school called St. Anthony's / quite near the docks.

78 ɪn θʎ́ɹd͡ʒ˺ ɪiəɹ | wɛn á wəz ɪn mɐ θʎ:d ɪíə ðə skǘɫ tɹanzféɪd
79 fɹəm ðaʔ bɪ́ldɪŋ ɪn ɫíθ ə tɒ̊ə ʌ bɹɪ́ɫjən? pɫés ət dʎ́dɪŋstn |
80 ün̩ d̥ə wé tə mʌ́sɫbʌɹʌʰ | əʔ ðə bɒ́ʔm· áɹθəɹz sí? áʔtʃəɫe ɪn
81 hólɪɹüd pák | nɔʔ fɑ́ɪ fɹəm hólɪɹüd páɹk ovəɹ ðɪ ʎ̈ðəɹ sǽɪd

In third year / when I was in my third year, the school
transferred from that building in Leith er to a brilliant
place at Duddingston / on the way to Musselburgh / at the
bottom of Arthur's Seat actually in Holyrood Park / not far
from Holyrood Park, over the other side.

82 wi θɔ́ʔ wi wüd kíp ɔn │ sɔɾ? ə │ a don no sʌ́m sɔɾ? ə hɨ́stəɾɨ

83 ə ðá? ném │ nʌ́ÿ ðə sɨ́?ɨz sʌ́əvb bæɪ tű kɔmpɾɨhénsɨv̥ ká̈θɨɨk

84 skű̈ɨz wʌ́n fəɾ̥ │ wɛ̥st sǽɪd wʌ́n fəɾ ð ís sǽɪd

    We thought we would keep on / sort of / I don't know, some
    sort of history of that name. / Now the city's served by
    two comprehensive Catholic schools, one for / west side,
    one for the east side.

85 ðəɪ̠s̠ mɔ́ɹ pɾʊ́tɨstənt skű̈z ɨn édɨnbʌɾʌ │ ðə pɾʊ́dɨstənt skű̈z

86 sim tə bi mɔ́ɾ ɨók̚ɨæɪzd │ sɛ́ɹ?n̩ dɨ́stɾɨks əv̥ ðə sɨ́tɨ

    There's more Protestant schools in Edinburgh / The Protes-
    tant schools seem to be more localized / certain districts
    of the city.

87 slá·ŋg̊ │ há·ŋ əɾʌ́ÿnd n ə gɾű̈p │ ma fá·ðəɾ jüs s ɔ́wɨz bi │

88 i jüs tˤ ɔ́wɨz tɛ̥́ɨ me tə stʊ́p sé̈ɨŋ má· ɨnstɛd əv̥ máɪ̥

    Slang / hang around in a group / My father used to always
    be / he used to always tell me to stop saying [ma·] instead
    of [maɪ].

89 píp̚ɨ ténd̚ tə │ spík moɾ ɨáɪk ðá·? │ nǽɪs tə tɔ́k̚ tə·

    People tend to / speak more like that / Nice to talk to.

90 mɔ́ə̇nɨnsæɪd ɨn édɨnbʌɾʌ jɛ· ðeɨ ɹɨfë̇ɹ të ðá·?

    Morningside in Edinburgh, yes, they'll refer to that.

91 wí tɛnd mi n̩ fɹénz ténd̚ tə ɾé̇çəɣnǽɪz ɨf sʌ́mbəde fɹö̇m ʌ

92 pɾívɪəsɨe pɾáɪvɨ? skű̈ɨ kʌ́mz̥ tə ðə ðɨs sékəndəɾe mɔ́dəɾn oɾ

93 kɔ́mpɾɨhénsɨv̥

    We tend, me and friends tend to recognize if somebody from
    a previously private school comes to the this secondary
    modern or comprehensive.

94 ðeɨ tɹáɪ ən ɾɨfʌ́ɪn ðeɾ̥ sɨá·ŋ kəɨók̊wɪəɨɨzmz̥

    They'll try and refine their slang colloquialisms.

95 ɨf jű gɔ́ fəɾ ən ɨ́n?ʌvjü fəɾ ə dʒɔ́·b │ sʌ́m píɸɨ ɐ nɔ́

    If you go for an interview for a job. / Some people I know.

88

(v) *Phonological discussion*
There are a number of characteristics of Edinburgh
speech which are quite different from those of the
other accents discussed in this book. The main ones
are: few, if any, contrasts between short and long
vowels; no clear [l]; use of /x/, with positional
variants [ç] and [x], which occurs not only in words
of Gaelic origin, e.g. *Drumsheugh*, but also in
English words: both speakers have [ç] in *recognize*,
even though lenition of intervocalic stops is not a
feature of this accent (see below); few diphthongal
articulations; consistent use of /h/; consistent use
of /ʍ/, though H has [w] in *when* on one occasion (78),
and the realizations [pɸ] (72) and [f] (76); rhot-
icity; no /ə/ element; a variety of v̆owel qualities
in unstressed syllables. The distinction between
/æɪ/ and /ʌɪ/, discussed by Wells (1982: 405-06),
does not appear to be relevant to either speaker, at
least with any consistency. G uses a diphthong in
the region of [æɪ‿aɪ], with one instance of [ɐɪ] in
outside (5); H has both types of articulation but
not exclusive to any particular context, e.g. [haɪ]
(64), [ʌɪ] (76), [bæɪ] (83); [ʌÿˀsʌɪd̥] (59), [ɨnsaed̥]
(63).

Another characteristic which marks off this
accent from the others discussed in this book is that
the major processes discussed in the Introduction
apply to a far lesser extent in both speakers.
H uses [ˀ] intervocalically for /t/, whereas G
does not; H also uses [ˀ] for /k/ before /t/.

(a) *Lenition*. There is little or no lenition of the
type, stop → fricative, or voiceless → voiced; H has
two examples of the former: [piɸö] *people* (55),
[rɛçəɣnæɪz] *recognize* (91), and one example of the
latter: [prɒdɨstənt̚] *Protestant* (55). The two sounds
that are affected most by lenition are /l/ and /r/.
G vocalizes or even deletes /l/ quite regularly, e.g.
[ɔö] *all* (14), [skuö] *school* (2) and (11), [sku:z]
schools (52) x 2, [odər] *older* (12). H, on the other
hand, does not usually°do so, though we must note
[piɸö] (55) and [ɔwɨz] *always* (87) and (88). In the
latter case we are dĕaling with /l/+/w/, the most
likely environment for vocalization, then deletion;
c.f. G's [sku wë] *school we* (11).

/r/, on the other hand, is vocalized and deleted
by both speakers in post-vocalic position. The flap,
with its slight closure phase, undergoes lenition
first to a frictionless continuant, then to a central
vowel [ə], then it is deleted, sometimes with a slight
effect on the preceding vowel, e.g.

G	H	
[mʌɹtʃənt] *merchant* (52)	────	frictionless continuant
[koət] *court* (3) [ʃɔət] *short* (42)	[sʌəvb] *served* (83)) [bɔən] *born* (73))	(slight) central vowel
[bʌdz] *birds* (38)(41)	[pɑk] *park* (81)	deletion
[ʌðəwaɪz] *otherwise* (48)	[ə] *or* (68)	deletion in unstres- sed syllable
[pɔʃʌ] *posher* (11)	[ɪnʔʌvjü] *interview* (95)	deletion + slight change in vowel quality
[fʌːst] *first* (21) [ʃɔ·t] *short* (47)	[θʌːd] *third* (78)))))	deletion + lengthen- ing of vowel.

We must note that some words occur both with and without any r-sound in the surface version, e.g. [bʌɹdz] (38), [θʌrd͡ʒ] (78), as well as the instances given above. It is most likely to be deleted before other post-alveolars, after the opening vowels /ʌ ɔ ɑ/, and finally in unstressed syllables. H has an example of intervocalic deletion: [d͡ʒüən] *during* (69). There are no examples of "intrusive" linking /r/. (For a discussion of /r/ in a number of Edinburgh children, see Romaine, 1978.)

(b) *Devoicing*. As in the previous locality, we find devoicing of voiced sounds, in particular fricatives and /r/, before voiced sounds, usually in word-final position, although G also devoices initial /ð/ after a devoiced final /ð/. E.g.

[wəz wɪð ðæt] *was with that* (2)

[ʍɛðər wɪð ðë] *whether with the* (8)

[ɑv afɛkteʃn] *of affectation* (14)

[hʌ̈yzɪz] *houses* (64)

[ɪɪv ðer] *live there* (65)

[wɪð ða·ʔ] *with that* (69).

Final devoicing before a pause also applies to vowels occasionally, e.g. [edɪnbrʌh] (51), [mʌsɪbʌrʌh] (71), (80), and /r/ is also affected in this way, e.g. [odər] (12), [ɹiəɾ] (78). Devoicing before voiceless

sounds, as in RP and most other accents, applies to
/r/, within the word, too, e.g. [wʌɾk] (26), (67)
and (69), and initial devoicing of ʔr/ occurs after
voiceless stops and fricatives, e.g. [fɹəm] (13) and
(62), [tres] (14). In one instance we find final
devoicing of a vowel before a voiceless sound:
[mɑ·hkədɫɪ] (31).

(c) *Harmony*. As with lenition, there is less
evidence of harmony in the speech of these two informants than is the case in other accents. The place
harmony of the alveolars displayed by most accents
(cf. Introduction, and Lodge, 1981) is much more
restricted in that it occurs most before the dentals
and rarely elsewhere, except in the case of /n/ +
velar (see below). For example:

 [bət̪ ðəz] *but there's* (9)

 [ət̪ ðə] *at the* (35)

 [ʌÿʔsʌɪd̪ ðə] *outside the* (59)

 [an̪ ðə] *on the* (59)

 [mʌn̪θs] *months* (61),

but [wʌn gɛts] (12), [ðən me] (73). G has one
example of /s/-harmony, giving [koɾθ ðə] *course the*
(14), but he has no harmonizing to bilabial or velar
articulations. H has a few examples, but they are
sporadic rather than regular:

 [kɔɫb mʌsɫbʌɾʌʰ] *called Musselburgh* (71)

 [sʌəvb bæɪ] *served by* (83).

In one case he has a double articulation: [θʌɾd͡ʒ ʒiəɾ]
(78), alongside non-harmonized [θʌːd ʒiə] (78). The
one regular harmony of a post-alveolar to velarity
is that of /n/ before /k/ and /g/ within the word,
e.g. [θɪŋk] (48), [ɪŋgɫənd] (22), but we must note
that it does not harmonize to bilabiality under the
same conditions, as can be seen from both speakers'
pronunciation of *Edinburgh*.

 Manner harmony is restricted to /ð/-harmony,
which is more common in H than in G, e.g.

 [ən̪ n̪æt̪ʔ] *on that* (23)

 [teks səm] *takes them* (47) + voice harmony

 [ɫn̪ n̪ə] *in the* (55)

 [ən̪ d̪ë] *on the* (67),

alongside the non-harmonized forms, one of which, *on
the* (59), is given above. There are no instances of

/ð/-harmony to /l/. H has two further instances of manner harmony, which are probably slips of the tongue rather than evidence of a phonological process, because of their unusual nature: [brʌðð] (76), [jüs s] (87).

Palatal harmony is more in evidence than the other types, though again there are occasions where it does not take place:

[aktʃeɫë] *actually* (5)

[ɛdʒükeʃn̩] *education* (9)

[ʌnjüʒɫ] *unusual* (43)

[aʔtʃeɫɨ] *actually* (65) and (80, with different final vowel)

[dʒüən̩] *during* (69),

but [ɨntɹədjüst] *introduced* (22)

[wəz jʌŋ] *was young* (72).

In one instance H has harmony between /l/ and a vowel: [ɫiθ] (79), where the vowel is retracted under the influence of the /l/-articulation.

(d) *CCS*. There are no examples of this in G's speech, but some in H's involving /t/ and /d/:

[fʌɹs θɹi] *first three* (61)

[is særd] *east side* (84)

[dɨstɹɨks] *districts* (86)

[fɹɛnz̥] *friends* (91).

There is one example of /t/-deletion after /n/: [don no] (82), but there is insufficient evidence for us to decide whether /-nt/ behaves differently from any other /-Ct/ or not (cf. the other localities above).

There is a /g/-deletion rule to produce morpheme-final [ŋ], and H has the alternative [-ɨn] ending for words ending in unstressed -*ing*, whereas G has not.

(e) *UVD*. Once again, this process is not as widely applied as in other accents. Within the word unstressed syllables are sometimes deleted, sometimes retained, e.g. G's [kʌmpənɪ] (52) versus H's [kʌmpne] (69). This is not a pattern distinguishing the two speakers, because we also have G's [nobdë] (17) versus H's [sɛkəndəɹe] (92). The first of two contiguous unstressed vowels is sometimes deleted:

[bɔʔm· aɹθ̩əɹz̥] *bottom of Arthur's* (80)

[ð ɪs] *the east* (84).

G has one example of reduction to a glide rather than deletion in [ðj ɐdmɪnɪstɹeʃn̩] (29-30).

(f) *Vowel lengthening.* /a/ is often lengthened, both where RP has /ɑ/ and elsewhere, especially before nasals, e.g.

[ɫaːft] *laughed* (3)

[haːmɫët] *hamlet* (6)

[səbstaːnʃəö] *substantial* (10)

[ðaːt aːksɛnt] *that accent* (10)

[ɹaːpɹdɫeʰ] *rapidly* (16)

[baːd] *bad* (16)

[aːfɹɪkən] *African* (40)

[aˑv] *I've* (62)

[ðaˑʔ] *that* (69), (89) and (90)

[faˑmɫe] *family* (76)

[aˑnθənɪz̥] *Anthony's* (77)

[haˑŋ] *hang* (87)

[faˑðəɾ] *father* (87).

In the case of speaker H the vowel phase is usually shorter than that of G. These are not just the environments involved in Aitken's Law (see Aitken, 1962; Ewen, 1977; and Wells, 1982: 405-06), though these, too, produce lengthening on occasion, e.g.

[fjüː] *few* (16)

[faˑɾ] *for* (17)

[kɔnfɛˑɹ] *confer* (32).

Some of the instances of lengthening may be the effect of stress in lento speech, e.g. [ɫɔˑts] (40) beside [ɫat] (22), [ɔˑd] (44), [dʒɔˑb] (95). In G's speech /e/ where it is equivalent to RP /e/ seems to be lengthened quite often, under a variety of circumstances, e.g.

[ɫeˑs] *less* (31)

[wikeˑnd] *week-end* (35)

[eˑg] *egg* (40)

[ənleˑs] *unless* (47).

Lastly, loss of /r/ also produces lengthening of the

preceding vowel phase, e.g.

    [fʌːst] *first* (21)

    [mɑ·hkədɫɪ] *markedly* (31)

    [mɑ·kt] *marked* (53)

    [θʌːd] *third* (78).

Chapter Five

COVENTRY

There is one male informant, A, aged 68. He was born
and educated in Coventry, but moved to Kenilworth at
the age of 12.

(i) *General*
This speaker has an articulatory setting which in
some respects resembles that of Liverpool speakers
(cf. Knowles, 1978: 89). The pharynx walls are
tightened and the faucal opening is quite narrow:
there is an adenoidal quality to much of his speech
(cf. Knowles, ibid.). The synchronization of velic
closure throughout the continuum does not always take
account of phonological segmentation. Consequently,
whole stretches of speech may be slightly, or even
heavily nasalized; on the other hand, nasal segments
are sometimes only nasal for half their duration, and
occasionally not nasal at all. The half-nasality I
have indicated by means of the appropriate non-nasal
letter with a tilde, e.g. [ã].
    /t d s z n/ are all post-alveolar, and the
fricative pair are not grooved, making them sound
very like /ʃ ʒ/. /t d n/ are usually dental before
/ð/. /l/ is always velarized.
    The voiceless stops are rarely aspirated, but
are often slightly affricated, especially /t/.
    Lip-rounding is produced by parting at the
centre only (cf. Stockport, above). It is widespread,
associated not only with the "rounded" vowels, but
with consonants and unstressed vowels too.

(ii) *Vowel diagrams*

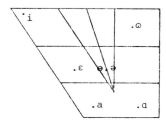

short monophthongs

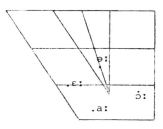

long monophthongs

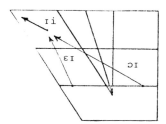

front closing
diphthongs

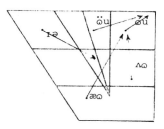

back closing
diphthongs
and [ɪə]

96

(iii) *The transcription*

1   jɛ ɔɪ jǔus t'av ə kózən | wɛn iʔ wəz̥ féːst ʌ̹ɒpm̩ ʃɪi wəz in̩

2   n̩ə káʃbɑks

    Yes, I used to have a cousin / when it was first open, she
    was in the cashbox.

3   gíi jəɾ éniθiɡ̃ tʃíip

    Give you anything cheap.

4   blʌ̹ʊkʔ kɒm ɹǽɒndʰ | ʃɤ̈vd ə káːd θɹɒu ðə dɔ́ː

    Bloke come round / shoved a card through the door.

5   bɒd̥ ðə wəz̥ sómbdi ɛ̃ɫs kɒm ð ɤ̈ðə dɛɪ ə wǒmən

    But there was somebody else come the other day, a woman.

6   ʃi kǒm wɔːɫ ɔ́ː wɔ́ːn̩ʔ n̩ɛ́ː

    She come while I wasn't there.

7   ä̈ɫ ɫəz ə fáːm ɣp an̩ n̩ə ɹɔ́ɪt' fɹəm m̩n̩ɛ́ː | bifɔ́ː ðə bɔ́ɪpas |

8   ən ɔɪ síi ðis | kǽɒdɒɡ | dʒɒst ʌ̹ʊvə ðə fɛ́ns | ən ä̈d gád ə |

9   litɫ sánbag wi mi | ö pǒd it' ít̚ d̥is sámbag wi gáɹ ä̈m bʰ bɒz̥

    Well, there's a farm up on the right from there / Before
    the by-pass / And I see this / cow dung / just over the
    fence / and I'd got a / little sand-bag with me. / I put it
    in this sand-bag, we got on the bus.

10   náʔ ɫaːst íistə ʃɔ́ːɫi

    Not last Easter, surely?

11   ʃi wɒn áːf

    She won't half.

12   iz záʔ ʔə t'ɛ́ɫifʌɒm báks | nɛks dɔ́ː

    Is that the telephone box / next door?

13   iʔ wəz nɛ́ks dɔ́ː tə ðáʔ wɛɹ áɫis wəz tɛ́kin ə fʌ̹ʊtṳ· insɔ́ɪd̥

14   ðatʔ

    It was next door to that, where Alice was taking a photo
    inside that.

15 ɔɪ stíɫ wɛ́:ɾ i? nǽɷ | na?s əβaɷ? | éɪtɹin íəɪ əgɷu

I still wear it now / and that's about eighteen year ago.

16 äɛv ad ə bɫɷ́u ən | ðə sɛ́ɪm sɔ́:t

I've had a blue one / the same sort.

17 djə ɹɛ́kən nəz̥ tɷ́u

Do you reckon there's two?

18 ən ɹi sɛ́z ɔ́ɪ wəz zə bɫʌ́ok əz əd: tɷ́g id ǽɷt | tɷ́u fɷ́t əv
19 ɛ́m mənɷ́uəɪ iṇ ṇat͇ táp fɫɫ́át͇

And he says, I was the bloke as had took it out / two foot of hen manure in that top flat.

20 iz dʒɔ́ɪs stiɫ ɫɛ́·

Is Joyce still there?

21 mɛ́ni ǽɷɪ ət͇ ḍát͇ | fɔ́ɪvstʌɷw̃: wɛn ɔ́ wəz ə kíd

Many hour at that / fivestones, when I was a kid.

22 dídntʃə tɛk nʌɷ fʌ́ɷtʌɷz əv ðát͇

Didn't you take no photos of that?

23 iz zá? ?ə sɛ́ɪm wán

Is that the same one?

24 ä bɔ́:t ɪ ə plánt əʒ̃ ʃi tʌ́ɷɫ mi ði ɷ́ðə wíɪk i cɫʌ́ɷziz in:
25 nɔ́ɪt ən kɷmz ǽɷt iṇ ṇə dɛ́ɪtɔɪm

I bought her a plant and she told me the other week, it closes in the night and comes out in the day-time.

26 ä́ dʌɷm? bḁ́ɾə tə ɹimɛ́mbə nɛ́ɪmz̥

I don't bother to remember names.

27 ä bɔ́:t ə θɪ́ɪi | iṇ ə pát | ən ʃi tɷ́g̊ ə ɫíif ɔ:f ðát

I bought her three / in a pot / and she took a leaf off that.

98

28 ɛ́:d ə ðə wíndə | ðɛɾ ɔ́: ɹɔ́ɪp˺ bɒt | ɔ̈ ɫɔ́:st ə ɫát əv əm

Out of the window / They're all right but / I lost a lot of them.

29 ä b˺ pɔ́ɹ ə ɫaɾ ə kɔ́tinz ín: páts bɒt̪˺ d̪ɛɪ: kɔ́m tə nɔ̃́θiŋg̊

I'd put a lot of cuttings in pots but they come to nothing.

30 jɒu kán kíɫ əm

You can kill them.

31 ä bɛ́ɾ iʒ ʒəɹɛ́ɪnjəmz əɹ | gɛ́ɾin ɹɛ́di nǽɷ nɪ́əli fə | pɫántin
32 ǽɒt | ɹiɫ av̥ fɫǽɷez a·n əm bifɔ́:ɾ ɹi pɔ́ts əm ǽɒt | ɹid ad
33 ɫá:ʃ ɹə

I bet his geraniums are / getting ready now nearly for / planting out. / He'll have flowers on them before he puts them out / He'd had last year.

34 sɒm pɪ́ŋkiɹ wɔ́nz | bɒt íz n jɒu sɹ́i iz gá:din | iɳ ðə
35 sɔ́mətɔɪm ən iz wán píktʃə | ɹi gɹʌ́ɷz bígis pá:t ɒn it
36 izsɛ́öf
   ̥

Some pinky ones / but his ... and you see his garden / in the summertime and it's one picture / He grows biggest part on it hisself.

37 ɛ́: dʒɑnz gá:din it stɹɛ́tʃiz fɹəm | fɹəm íə ti· ðə bák˺ gɛ́ɪt

Our John's garden it stretches from / from here to the back gate.

38 ʃɹi dídn̩ kɒm íw̃ wán dɛɪ
         ˈ
She didn't come in one day.

39 əɹ ɷ́zbən jɔ́ust˺ bi aɳ ɳə kəmíti ɷp ðə cɫɷ́b jɹəz ən jɹəz əgɔ́u

Her husband used to be on the committee up the club years and years ago.

40 ðəz tɔ́u sɹ́iɫinz ä wán im tə dɔ́u wán iɳ ɳə fɹɔ́n? bɛ́dɹɷum əw̃
                                                              ̥
41 wan iɳ ɳə | mídɫ ɹɷum dǽɒnstɛ́:z
                                ̥
There's two ceilings I want him to do, one in the front bed-room and one in the / middle room downstairs.

42 ä wέn ε:ʔ n̩ fɹɔ́ɪdɹi | ən á:θəz bέ:θdεɪ

I went out on Friday / on Arthur's birthday.

43 ɹi έĩ̃ʔ bin dǽɔn wɪð ə | bɔɾ ɹiz vέɾi vεɾi kwɔ́ɪət

He ain't been down with her / but he's very, very quiet.

44 əz ʌɔni θɹíi ä́m əm

There's only three on them.

45 jɔβ sín dʒánz εĩ̃ʔ jə | wεɫ jɔ sin wán əv əm

You've seen John's, ain't you? / Well, you seen one of them.

46 wεɫ ɔ́:ɫ áv it̚ʔ | a gaɾ ə fɔ́ɪn sɔ́mmõni nǽɔ tə kɔm ən töun it |

47 i wants töunin | i sε d̠iʔ pjánə ɾɔnə á:f wanʔ töunin

Well, I'll have it. / I got to find somebody now to come and
tune it / it wants tuning / He said, This piano doesn't half
want tuning.

48 ä ʃá:mʔ bɑ́ðə

I shan't bother.

49 tʃápiw̃ wɔ́d ən: ðá́ʔ | ən̩ n̩έm wεn ɔ̈ lέf skɔuɫ ɔ̈ wεn̩ʔ n̩ε:

50 pέ:mənənt

Chopping wood and that / and then when I left school I went
there permanent.

51 ən ä wέn in̩ n̩i áfis | ən ä jɔsᵗ sə gɔ́u wi ði ɔ́:siz | ɔ̈ jɔs

52 də ɹɔ́ɪd̠ʔ d̠ə tʃέɪnɔ:s

And I went into the office / and I used to go with the
horses / I used to ride the chain-horse.

53 ðə fɹɔ̃́w̃ʔ w̃ɔ̃n

The front one.

54 ə big fɔ́ɪə dæɔn̩ n̩έ: á:ʰtə wi wə máɹid n̩ its ɔ́:ɫ gɑt̚ʔ bə:nt

55 ǽɔt

A big fire down there after we were married and it's all
got burnt out.

100

56 sɛptémbə twɛ̃di fɔ́ɪv | i wə bɔːt ɷ́p wɪð əm | dʒɔ́ːdʒ bɔːt ím

57 ɷp

September '25 / He were brought up with m / George brought
him up.

58 mi áːnti ad ʔǽɷs | ðɛ́ː ən̪ ðə dɹɔ́ɪv wɛnd ɷp íə

My auntie had a house / there, and the drive went up here.

59 əkɹɔ́ːs zə ɹʌ̊ɷ̊ψ fɹəm ðɛ́m | wɛɫ ɛɪ wə bʌ̊ɷθ əkɹɔ́ːs zə ɹʌɷd

Across the road from them / Well, they were both across the
road.

60 mi dád wəz in̪ n̪ə tə́im

My dad was in the team.

61 ðə wɪ́k̚ bifɔ́ː wid̚ bin pɫɛ́ɹin̪ n̪ə ɫ́idʒən

The week before we'd been playing the Legion.

62 if jɷ́ kʰ bïit ím | wi kũ wín̪ n̪ís

If you can beat him / we can win this.

63 ɔɪ θín̪g̊ ik̚ kɔ́ːs mi tɛ́n pǽɷnd

I think it cost me ten pound.

64 ðə jɷ́us tə bɹi ə ʃáft | ɹɷ́nin̪ θɾɷ́u | ði ǽɷziz

There used to be a shaft / running through the houses.

65 f äĩ̩ŋ gə́nə stáp mb fɔ̃ĩm mĩ wɛɪ nǽɷ ɔɪ θĩ́ŋk ɔɪ ʃɷb̚ bi ɫáss |

66 ɔ́ː ɫə ɹɛ́st wə dʒɛ́st | stɹɛ́ɪt æɷt ántə ðə páθ

If I'm going to stop and find my way now, I think I should
be lost / All the rest were just / straight out onto the
path.

67 ðə wz ʌɷni mɹi ðíə də ɫɷk áːtə mi mɷ́ðə

There was only me there to look after my mother.

68 bɷʔ d̪ə sɛ́ɪm píipɫ kɛ́p it | əz kɛ́p it | wɛ̃ mɷ́ðə wəz ə kíd

But the same people kept it / as kept it / when mother was
a kid.

69 káptin áːst im də gə dǽon̥ ðə ɬɔ́ɪw̃ wóns

    Captain asked him to go down the line once.

70 ðə báːθɹɷum wəz zə fés dʒab

    The bathroom was the first job.

(iv) *Phonological discussion*
This accent can be seen as sharing some characteristics with more northerly ones and some with southern
ones (cf. Wells, 1982: 363); thus, there is no /ɷ/-
/ʌ/ distinction, but words with the diphthong of
time have a realization [ɔɪ] (and there may be no
distinction between *buy* and *boy*, cf. Wells, ibid.).
Also there is fluctuation between [a] and [aː], [ɑ]
and [ɔː] before voiceless fricatives (see below).
/h/ does not occur, nor does syllable-final /r/.
There is inconsistent use of final [ŋ] and [ŋg̊] (see
below).
    The definite article is often omitted as a
result of a number of processes, as exemplified below;
there is no evidence of the glottal stop realization,
as found in Stockport (see Chapter 1).

(a) *Lenition*. The most common lenition applies to
voiceless stops, which are either realized as lenes
or completely voiced, usually in intervocalic position, but also elsewhere, e.g.

    [bɒd̥ ðə] *but the* (5)

    [tɷg̊ ə] *took a* (27)

    [jɷs d̥ə] *used to* (51-52)

    [θiŋg̊] *think* (63)

    [gɑd ə] *got a* (8)

    [tɷg id æɷt] *took it out* (18)

    [ɛːd ə] *out of* (28)

    [wɛnd ɷp] *went up* (58).

Flaps are sometimes used, e.g. [gɛɾin] *getting* (31),
[pjanə ɾɷnə] *piano doesn't* (47), and lenition to a
frictionless contunuant also takes place, e.g. [gɑɹ
äm] *got on* (9). Occasionally, lenition from stop to
fricative takes place, e.g. [əβaɷʔ] *about* (15).
Vocalization and deletion of /l/ are not common, e.g.

    [ɔː ɹɔɪp̚] *all right* (28)

    [izsɛöf] *hisself* (36).

(b) *Harmony*. As in the other accents, the commonest sounds which undergo place harmony are the alveolars, e.g.

[bɷd̪ ðə] *but the* (5)

[ɑ̈m b˺ bɷz̥] *on the bus* (9)

[ɛm mənɷuəɹ] *hen manure* (19)

[n̪ɛm wɛn] *then when* (49)

[ɹʌɷɸ fɹəm] *road from* (59).

There are exceptions and variation, e.g.

[tɛn pæɷnd] *ten pound* (63)

[ən kɷmz] *and comes* (25)

[didn̩ kɷm] *didn't come* (38)

[fɹɷn? bɛd-] *front bed-* (40)

and [sanbag] alongside [sambag] *sandbag* (9). [ɑ̈m əm] *on them* (44) is an example of non-contiguous harmony which seems to be exceptional. There is one example of /m/ harmonizing its place of articulation: [ɑ̈ĩŋ gənə] *I'm going to* (65). In the case of [stɑp mb fɔ̃ĩm] *stop and find* (65) the syllabic masal and' following stop harmonize with the preceding consonant, not the following one.

Palatization of /t d s z/ also occurs:

[didn̩tʃə] *didn't you* (22)

[iʒ ʒɵɹɛɪnjɵmz] *his geraniums* (31)

[ɫa:ʃ ɪə] *last year* (33),

though there is one instance where it does not apply: [djə] (17).

/ð/ harmonizes as to manner, even to an oral stop after a stop, e.g.

[in̪ n̪ə] *in the* (1-2)

[wɔ:n̪? n̪ɛ] *wasn't there* (6)

[ɑ̈ɫ ɫəz] *well, there's* (7)

[fɹəm m͡n̪ɛ̃:] *from there* (7)

[it̪ˀ˺ d̪is] *in this* (9)

[ɑ̈m b˺ bɷz̥] *on the bus* (9)

[iz za? ?ə] *is that the* (12) and (23)

[ət̪ˀ˺ d̪at] *at that* (21)

[bɷ? d̪ə] *but the* (68).

In [sɛ d̥i?] *said this* (47) Geminate Simplification
has been applied. In one instance we have an alveolar nasal (and no unstressed vowel) for the definite
article: [in: nɔɪt] (24-25), and in another case a
flap articulation is used: [baɾə] *bother* (26). There
is also one instance of devoicing following /s/:
[əkɪɔ:s z̥ə] (59).
Manner harmony, with place harmony as appropriate,
also applies to the alveolars, e.g.

[iw̃ wan] *in one* (38)

[fɪɔ̃w̃? w̃ɔ̃n] *front one* (53)

[kũ̥ wiṇ] *can win* (62).

In [əz̃ ʃi] *and she* (24), palatal harmony has not taken
place. /t/ harmonizes to a fricative after /s/ occasionally:

[jɒsᵗ sə] *used to* (51)

[ɬass] *lost* (65).

In [fɔɪvstʌɒw̃: wɛn] *fivestones when* (21) both /n/ and
/z/ harmonize with the following /w/.
    Nasalization and denasalization have already been
mentioned above as a general phonetic feature of this
speaker. In some instances nasality occurs as a consequence of the deletion of the stop feature of /n/,
as in the case of other accents, e.g. [ɛɪ̃?] *ain't* (43)
and (45), but there are also instances where nasality
occurs over a considerable number of segments, e.g.

[sɒmm̃ɔ̃ni] *somebody* (46)

[fɪɔ̃w̃? w̃ɔ̃n] *front one* (53)

[fɔ̃ɪ̃m mɪ̃] *find me* (65).

(c) *CCS*. This applies to /t/ and /d/, as in the
other accents, in morpheme-final position followed
by another consonant, e.g.

[nɛks dɔ:] *next door* (12)

[tʌɒɬ mi] *told me* (24)

[bigis pa:t] *biggest part* (35)

[fɔ̃ɪ̃m mɪ̃] *find me* (65).

/k/, too, is deleted in the context /s/___C, e.g.
[a:st] *asked* (69). In one instance the /d/ of initial
/dʒ/ is deleted: [iʒ ʒəɪɛɪnjəmz] (31), but this may
be exceptional.
    The modified version of Geminate Simplification,
discussed above in Peasmarsh, in which two matched

place features trigger the deletion of the second
segment containing the matched feature (which would
seem to have to be alveolar), appears to operate in
A's speech, as in:

[wɒn] *wouldn't* (11)

[didn̩] *didn't* (38)

[ɒzbən] *husband* (39)

[wɑn] *want* (40)

[wɛn] *went* (42) and (51).

That this is not CCS operating is demonstrated by the
fact that, with the exception of the examples at (38)
and (39), a vowel follows. There is one instance
where the final /t/ is not deleted but voiced: [wɛnd
ɒp] *went up* (58). There are no examples of left-to-
right Nasal Harmony, resulting in [nn], as in Shepherd's Bush and Peasmarsh.

In other instances Geminate Simplification
applies as in the other accents, e.g.

[ɔ: ɫə] *all the* (66)

[wɛ̃ mɒðə] *when mother* (68).

Final [ŋ] occurs without a following [g], but
also with both nasal and oral stop articulations,
even before a pause: compare [-dɒŋ] (8) with [nɒθiŋg̊]
(29). /g/-deletion also applies, as in [tö̈unin] (49),
[tʃɑpiw̃ wɒd] (49), with Manner Harmony as well in the
latter example.

(d) *UVD*. Unstressed vowels are deleted when two
vowels come together across word-boundaries, e.g.

[t av] *to have* (1)

[ð ɒðə] *the other* (5).

Often, when the stress pattern is $\acute{V}C_n\breve{V}C_n\breve{V}$, where C_n
may be one or more consonants, the middle vowel is
deleted, as in:

[sɒ́mbdi] *somebody* (5)

[bɔ́:t ɪ ə] *bought her a* (24)

[jɒ́ustˀ bi] *used to be* (39).

Even with other stress patterns, deletion occurs,
e.g.

[in: nɔ́ɪt] *in the night* (24-25)

[ad ʔǽɒs] *had a house* (58)

[ðə wz ʌɔni] *there was only* (67).

Utterance-initial unstressed vowels disappear occasionally, as in: [f äĩŋ] *If I'm* (65).

(e) *Vowel lengthening*. Before voiceless fricatives there is fluctuation in the application of lengthening, even in the same word, e.g.

[ɔːf] (27)   [ʃaft] (64);
[ɫɔːst] (28)   [ɫass] (65);
[baːθ-] (70)   [paθ] (66).

Before /-nC/ there seems to be no lengthening: [pɫantin] (31).

(f) *Linking r*. Linking r is used, sometimes as a flap, even when there is no underlying /r/; sometimes it does not occur, though, e.g.

[jəɾ ɛniθiɣ̃] *you anything* (3)
[ɪəɹ əgɔu] *year ago* (15)
[ɾɔnə aːf] *doesn't half* (47).

(g) *Derivations*. To demonstrate the interaction of the processes, I give three sample derivations below, two of which show how the definite article is reduced and deleted:

/an ðɪi bɔz/

Stress placement	⟹	än ðə bɔ́z
UVD	⟹	än ð bɔ́z
/ð/-harmony	⟹	än b bɔ́z
Place harmony	⟹	[äm b bɔ́z̥] (9).

/wɛn mɔðr̩ + C/

Stress placement	⟹	wɛn mɔ́ðr̩ C-
/r/-realization	⟹	wɛn mɔ́ðə C-
Nasalization	⟹	wɛ̃n mɔ́ðə
Place harmony	⟹	wɛ̃m mɔ́ðə
Geminate simplif.	⟹	[wɛ̃ mɔ́ðə] (68).

```
          /gɹʌɒz ðɪi bigist/
Stress placement    =    gɹʌɒz ðə bígist
/ ð/-harmony        =    gɹʌɒz zə bígist
Geminate Simplif.   =    gɹʌɒz ə bígist
UVD                 =    [gɹʌɒz bígis]  (35),
```

where CCS removes the final /t/ of *biggest*.

Chapter Six

NORWICH

There is one informant, E, male, aged 68. He was
born in Norwich and has lived there all his life.

(i) *General*
For a detailed description of the articulatory
setting of many Norwich speakers, see Trudgill (1974:
185-91). E has a relatively tense musculature,
occasional stretches of creaky voice, particularly
in the neighbourhood of glottal stops, and sometimes
his low, front vowels are nasalized slightly.
The voiceless stops are usually, but not always
aspirated in syllable-initial position, and /t/ is
often affricated as well. /l/ takes on the quality
of the following vowel in word-initial position, so
that, for example, [lɛf] *left*, [lɨʔɫ] *little* and
[ɫʊk] *look* all have slightly different qualities in
the first sound.
Lip-rounding is not particularly marked except
in /ɔː/. It is associated with the bilabial sounds,
giving a slight rounded quality to a following back
vowel, as indicated in the transcription, and /ɑɪ/
after other sounds too, such as /l/ and /r/, is sometimes realized as [ɒɪ].
Glottal reinforcement of the voiceless stops is
used, even in intervocalic position. The synchronization of the two closures varies to some extent,
but I have not indicated this below.
The amount of retraction of the tongue for /r/
varies, as indicated in the difference between [ɹ]
and [ɹ̠]; in one instance a retroflex tap is used:[ɾ].
The rhythm of Norwich speech is unlike that of
the other accents discussed in this book. The
quantity of both stressed and unstressed vowels
varies considerably, and length of both monophthongs
and diphthongs in stressed syllables may be considerable (cf. Wells, 1982: 341).

108

(ii) *Vowel diagrams*

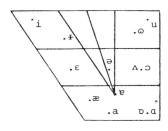

short monophthongs

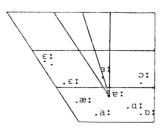

long monophthongs

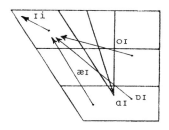

front closing
diphthongs

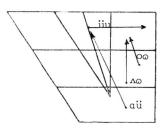

back closing
diphthongs and [aü]

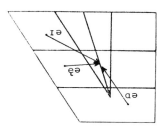

centring diphthongs

109

(iii) *The transcription*

1 ɨf áɪ wɛnt̚ t'ə ðə l̲ɨ́ˀɫ vɨ̲l̲ɨdʒəz áü̃ˀsaɪd ná:ɹ̲ɨdʒ | dɹ̲ǽ̃ɪˀn

2 t'ǽɪvɹəm ɛ́nɨwɛ: ɫaɪˀ ðǽ:ˀ | aɪ æd əbáü̃ˀ ə θɹ̲íi maɪɫ kʌ̃́nˀɹi

3 wɔ́:k̚ tə gɛ́t̚ tɚ:m | ən wɔ́ns aɪ gá:ˀ ðɛ: | ðeɪ nṹu aɪ wəz ə

4 sɨ́ˀi kɨd əz̥ sunz ɛ́vɹ aɪ ó̃ɷp̲mz mə mã́üθ

    If I went to the little villages outside Norwich / Drayton,
    Taverham, anywhere like that / I had about a three-mile
    country walk to get to them / And once I got there / they
    knew I was a city kid as soon as ever I opens my mouth.

5 ðə dɨ́fˀəns twɨ̥n ðə ná:ɹ̲ɨdʒ dá́əɫəkt ən̥ n̥ə nɔ́:fək̚ dá́əɫəkt wəz

6 t'əɹ̲ɨ́fɨk

    The difference between the Norwich dialect and the Norfolk
    dialect was terrific.

7 ðæɪ wɛnˀ ɨ́nˀəɹ̲ ə ʃá:p̚ˀ tə bóɪ sʌ́fɪ̃ŋ

    They went into a shop to buy something.

8 ðæɪ wəɹ̲ ǽ:pɨˀ

    They were happy.

9 aɪ gá:ˀ ʌp̚ ə l̲ɨ́ˀɫ bɨ̸ˀ ʃá:pɨʃ ən aɪ k'ɔ́:ˀ maɪ ɛ́d a·n ə bɨ́ˀ ə

10 p'óɪp̚

    I got up a little bit sharpish and I caught my head on a bit
    of pipe.

11 wɛ̈ ɫə bɫó̃k̚ˀ nɛ́ks tüu mɨ wəz ə sɨ́ˀi bɫɷk̚

    Well, the bloke next to me was a city bloke.

12 ðæɪg gɨ́v əm ə pó̃k̚ˀ ə ðə ɫʌ́g əz̥ sunz zæɪd ɫõ̥k̚ˀ æ̲:ˀ ə̃m

    They'd give them a poke at the lug as soon as they'd look at them.

13 ða̠ˀ wəz ðə ɹʌ́fəs p'ɫɛ̠́:s ðɛ: wɛ́̃z̥

    That was the roughest place there was.

14 ən̥ n̥ə bɹ́im wɒˀ wɛnˀ əkɹɔ́:st ad ðə jó̃ɷɫᵈz dɹɨ́ɫd ɨn əˀ wɛ: ði

15 oɷɫ ɫó:m jüus tə fɨ́ks

    And the beam what went across had the holes drilled in it
    where the old loom used to fix.

16 ðæɪ ɔ́:ɫwɪst ǽd ən ɪnvé:ʔəd ɔ́:ʃüu ǽ:ŋɪn oꞷvə ðə fɪʌ́n? dɔ́: fə

17 lʌ́·k

They always had an inverted horse-shoe hanging over the
front door for   luck.

18 tʃʌ́x ə? oꞷvə jə léf ʃʌꞷɫdə | ən wɔ́:k˺ kwʊ́ɪəʔli əwǽɪ wɪðɑ́ü?

19 ɫǿkt̩ biʊ́ɪnd

Chuck it over your left shoulder / and walk quietly away
without looking behind.

20 mʊ́ɪnd ʒǘu | ɪf jǘu ɔ́:d˺ gɫá:s əbɪɛ́:kən á:ftə jüud˺ tʃʌ́kt̪ ðæ?

21 óꞷvə jɔ: ʃʌꞷɫdə | jüud˺ pǿɾ ə? θɪüu sʌ́mwʌnᵈz wɪ́ndə

Mind you / if you heard glass a-breaking after you'd
chucked that over your shoulder / you'd put it through
someone's window.

22 wɛ́n̩ n̩i ʌ́ꞷɫ dévəɫ ɫʊ́k˺ dɑ́ün̩ n̩ə tʃɪ́mnɪ | ən sɔ́: ðæ? pɔ́ɪn? ə

23 ðǽ:? p˹ǿkə p˹ǿkən ʌ́p ǽ:? ə̃mn̩ | ɪ́ibˑbi ɑ́ü? ðæ? tʃɪ́mĪɪ p˹ɑ́:?

24 ɫʊɪk˺ gɪɪ́iz ɫʊ́ɪʔnən | ǽ:n̪d̪ ði ʌ́ꞷɫ fɑ́·ɪ əd stá:? dɪɔ́:ɪən

When the old devil looked down the chimney / and saw that
point of that poker poking up at him / he'd be out of that
chimney pot like grease lightning / And the old fire would
start drawing.

25 ən ɫʊkt' á:ʔəɪ ə? | nóꞷbɒ·di ɪn ði ɑ́üs əd évə wʊ́:n?

And looked after it / nobody in the house would ever want.

26 fɪəm ɛ́: ʔɪ | maüsʌꞷɫd ən n̩ n̩a? wǿn̩? ə bɪɔ́:k

From here to / Mousehold and that wouldn't have broke.

27 jü dɪn? æv t˹ɑ́ɪŋ fə nóꞷ bɪɛ́:kfəst | ən aʒ jü wɔ́:kt əɫɑ́:ŋ ðɛ́

28 wəʒ jǘʒəɫi ə k˹ʌ́ꞷɫ nɪ́p ɪn̩ n̩i ɛ́: | əm bə ðə t˹ɑ́ɪm jü gɑ́:t̪

29 ðɛ· jü won? á:f ʌ́:ŋgɪɪ

You didn't have time for no breakfast / and as you walked
along, there was usually a cold nip in the air / and by the
time you got there, you weren't half hungry.

30 wɔnʃ jüud˺ tɛ́:stɪd ɪz ɪɔ́s tɛ́:ʔəz | ðass sʌ́fən jüud ɪɪmémbə

31 fə ðə ɪést ə jə ɫʊ́ɪf | ðæɪ wə bǘuʔəfɫ

111

Once you'd tasted his roast taters / that's something you'd
remember for the rest of your life / They were beautiful.

32 ən i nṹ əʔ ɔ́:ɬ ɔ́:f bəɹ̱ ɑ́:ʔ

And he knew it all off by heart.

33 mɒ́st ə ði ʌɷɬ wɪ́ivz əɗ tén ʔ ʔə ʃṹumɛ̰́:kən

Most of the old weavers had turned to shoemaking.

34 ɹid sʌ́mtɐmz goɷ dɑ́ün ʔə wɔ́:ʔə lɛ̰́:n stǽɪð ən t'ɔ́:k̚ tə̰ɹ̱ ɛ́nɨ
35 ði ʌɷɬ wɛ́ɹ̱mən

He'd sometimes go down to Water Lane Staithe and talk to
any of the old wherrymen.

36 p'ɪ̰́k ʌp stʌ́f ɔ:f ðə fɑ́:ɹ̱ən bɷ́ts wɒ ʔ pɷ ʔ ɪ̰n̪ ðɛɹ̱ ən bɹɪ̰ŋ ə ʔ
37 ɔ́:ɬ bǽ:k̚ dɑ́ün ʔə nɑ́:ɹ̱ɨdʒ̰

Pick up stuff off the foreign boats what put in there and
bring it all back down to Norwich.

38 ɹi wəz go ʔə sɛ̰́:v ʌp ɔ́:ɬ ɨz mɒ́nɨ

He was going to save up all his money.

39 ɑ́:ɹ̱ɨk'ɑ́ʔ bɪ́inz wɨð ə bɪ̰ ʔ ə bɛ̰́:çən bɷ́əɬd ɨn wɪ̰·ð ə ʔ | kos
40 sæɪ dɪ̰́ʔn̩ ɹi ʔ ðə bɛ̰́:çən ðə sǽɪm dǽɪ | ða ʔ wz ʌɷnɨ fɬɛ̰́:vəɹ̱ən

Haricot beans with a bit of bacon boiled in with it /
Course they didn't eat the bacon the same day / That was
only flavouring.

41 ɹi ǽt̚ t'ə goɷ dɑ́ün gʌ́ɷɬdən dɔ:g lɛ̰́:n | ðɛ̈ wəz ən ʌ́ɷɬd ɹṹənɗ
42 tʃɛ́tʃ ɑ́:f wæɪ dɑ́ün | ɹi wz ʌɷni bɑü ʔ sɛ́vən əɹ̱ ǽɪ ʔ | ən ɨ
43 jüs tə ʔɑ́:p əɬɑ́:ŋ

He had to go down Golden Dog Lane. / There was an old
ruined church half way down / He was only about seven or
eight / and he used to hop along.

44 ðɛ̈ wəz wɒ́n stɒ́n̩ ṉɛ́: | ə bɪ̰ ʔ bɪ̰́gɹ̱ ən ɔ́:ɬ ɬə ɹɛst

There was one stone there / a bit bigger than all the rest.

45 ɒɪ nɛ́vəɹ̱ ɜ́:ɖ ðǽ ʔ wɐd əfɔ́: | soɷ ʔɹi dɪ̰́dn ʔ bɑ́:ðə ʔ ɑ́:sk

112

I never heard that word afore / So he didn't bother to
ask.

46 ðɛm ɫɔ́vɫɨ gʌ̂ɵɫ lɛ́ʔəz | ɹʉ́ɪʔ əkɹɔ́:s ðə stɹɪ́i̯ʔ
    Them lovely gold letters / Right across the street.

47 fə sʌ́fᵵ ʔ ɪ́i̯ʔ | ʃɨ wəz ə ɹʌ́f ʌɵɫ gɛ́ɫ | ðæɪ ɛɗ p'ɫɛ́ʔi ə
48 t'ɑ́ɪm
    For something to eat / She was a rough old girl / They had
    plenty of time.

49 ʌ́ŋkɫ ɔ́:bə ʔ ɔ́:ɫwəz gɑ ʔ ʔɑ́:n ʔ ʔɑ́:ɹiə ʔs kɹɨ́sməs pɹɛ́zən ʔ ɔ:f ɔ́:
    Uncle Herbert always got Aunt Harriet's Christmas present
    off her.

50 ɨ gɑ ʔ ɹɛ́:znz ən ɨ spɹɛ́d̪ ðɹiz ɹɛ́:znz ɔ́:ɫ ɵꞷvə ðə t'ɨ́n tɹǽɪ
    He got raisins and he spread these raisins all over the tin
    tray.

51 soꞷ ɪi ɔ́:ɫəs sʌ́ŋ ə k'ʌ́nʔɹɨ sɑ́:ŋ
    So he always sung a country song.

52 ɛ́vɹɨ t'ɑɪm n̥ə k'é̞ʔənz k'ʌm dɑ́ün ðɛ̈ wəz nnʌ́ðə p'ɨ́ktʃə jüus
53 tə k'ʌ́m əkɹɔ́:st
    Every time the curtains come down, there was another
    picture used to come across.

54 mɑ́ün ʔ vəsʉ́uviəs ɨn əɹʌ́ptʃn̥ | ɛ́nɨbɑ·dɨ xəɗ gɵ́ꞷ ɨn ən wʉ́:tʃ
    Mount Vesuvius in eruption / Anybody could go in and watch.

55 ʃɪi æd lɛ́gz zə sɛ́:m əz ɛ́nɨwɔn ɛ́ɫs zaʔ wəz é̞: ɹəfɫɛ́kʃən ɨn̥
56 ðə k'ǽ:bnə ʔ
    She had legs the same as anyone else, that was her
    reflection in the cabinet.

57 ɨ jüs ʔ ə goꞷ ɑ́ü ʔ tə fǽɫθɔːp wɵ́dz | gǽðəɹ ɛ́:əðə
    He used to go out to Felthorp Woods / gather heather.

58 jə dɨʔn̥ nʌꞷ ɛ́: ðɛɪɗ bɨ́n dɨ́d ʒə

                                                        113

You didn't know where they'd been, did you?

59 ən əvéntʃɨɨ ða? fɨɜ́: fɑ́·ɪə

And eventually that flew afire.

60 ɪi pɔ́ɪn?ə t'ə mɪ́i ɪi sǽɪ | júu ɨn? gɑ́:? ə ɨʋ́ɪ?

He pointed to me, he say / You ain't got a light.

61 ðə gɹɑ́ünd stɑ́?t sʌ́dənɨɨ ðɛ: ən ðɛ́ wəz ə stɨ́ip ɨŋkɨʋɪn̥ nɛn ə

62 ɹɔ́: ə t'ɛ́ɹəst ɑ́üzəz

The ground stopped suddenly there and there was a steep
incline then a row of terraced houses.

63 ən ?ɛ́vɹi ɑ́:f dǽɪ | ɨg gɔ́ɷ ? ɹə dɨfɹən? skɔ́ɷɨ n̥ t'ɛ́:k˥ t'ú ə

64   θɹɪ́i dɨfɹəŋ? kɨɑ́:səz

And every half-day / he'd go to a different school and take
two or three different classes.

65 ɨn̥ ðə k'ɔ́:s əv ə jɛ́: jə lɑ́:s t'üu jɛ́əz ə? skɔ́ɷɨ jə gɑ́?

66 əbɑü? θɹɪ́i ɔ fɔ́: dɹɔ́:ɹən lɛ́sənz ə jɛ́ə

In the course of a year your last two years at school you
got about three or four drawing lessons a year.

67 ðæɪ ɔ́:ɨ ɛd ə t'ɑ́: wɨð ə bɛ́ɨ ɨn

They all had a tower with a bell in.

68 ʋɪ θɨŋg̊ ?a? wz ə k'ɨ́ɨ ɔ: k'ɔ́: düu ɹɛ́əɨɨ | ɨn̥ n̥ə sɔ́:mə

I think that was a kill or cure do, really / In the summer.

69 ðə t'ɹɪ́its jüus tə kɨɑ́:ʃ | ɑ:n ə θɜ́:zdɪ ɑ:f?nɔ́n

The treats used to clash / on a Thursday afternoon.

70 lɨ́?ɨ ɔ́ɷɨz ɨn̥ n̥ə bǽ:k ə ðɨ é·ɪɨz | ɪ́i jüs tə səpɨʋ́ɪ ɔ:ɨ ɨə

71 mət'ɛ́:ɹɨəɨz | ən ɹi kɨɹ́əd̥ ðɛm ɔ́:ɨ ɑü? | ðə wɔ́mən ʃɹʌ́k ɑ́ü?

Little holes in the back of the heels. / He used to supply
all the materials. / And he cleared them all out. / The
woman shruck out.

114

72 ðæɪ t'ɒ́? mɪ́ ʔə ðə dʒɛ́·nə lɪ̱nd ɑ́ü?p'ɛ́:ʃən?s dɪp'á:?mən? ɪn

73 pʊ́:dɪgə?

They took me to the Jenny Lind out-patients department in Pottergate.

(iv) *Phonological discussion*
This speaker's phonological system is quite different in many respects from those of the other informants. The vowel system has more distinctions, reflecting earlier stages of English. Thus the following distinctions are made, though it must be pointed out that not all speakers in Norwich necessarily make them, especially the younger generations.

(a) /æɪ/ in *staithe* versus /ɛ̞:/ in *lane*. The latter is kept distinct from /ɛ:/ in *there, here* (see (d) below).
(b) /üu/ in *through* versus /oʊ/ in *go, school, no* versus /ʌʊ/ in *shoulder*.
(c) Some reflexes of ME ē̠ may be retained in words like *heel* with [e·ɪ] (70), as opposed to /ɪi/ in *three* (64).
(d) /ɪə/ and /ɛ:/ are kept apart, though there is some inconsistency in the realization of the former, e.g. [kɫɪəd̠] *cleared* (71), [ɛ:] *air* (28), but [jɛ:] (65) and [jɛ̞ə] (66) *year*, and [mət'ɛ̞:ɹɪəɫz] *materials* (71). *Here* (26) is pronounced with a slightly closer variety of vowel than *air* (28), making it the same as the vowel in *lane* (34). (For further comments on this distinction, see Trudgill and Foxcroft, 1978: 76-77.)
(e) /ɜ:/ has a variant /ɐ:/: compare *her* on lines (49) and (55), note also [ɪnvɐ:?əd] *inverted* (16). However, most words with /ɜ:/ in RP and other accents in E's speech have a short /ɐ/. There is no evidence to suggest that this is a synchronic vowel shortening process in that there are no alternant pronunciations, long : short.

The distribution of vowels in lexical items also varies more here than in the other accents. For example, /ʊ/, as in *put*, is also found in *boat, roast, poke, poker, bloke, most* and *stone* (cf. Trudgill, 1974: 72-73). Here again there is no evidence of a synchronic shortening. /a:/ occurs in *Harriet's* (49) and *clash* (69), as well as in the expected *last* and *heart*. In one instance *same*, which elsewhere has /ɛ̞:/, has the diphthong found in younger speakers in

115

such words: [sæɪm dæɪ] *same day* (40). This could
well be influence of the more recent pronunciation
and the diphthong of the following word.
The glottal stop is a frequent realization of
/t/, even in initial position of an unstressed syllable, e.g. [ʔə] *to* (33), (34), (37), (38), (72). On
one occasion it occurs for /ð/: [ʔaʔ] *that* (68). It
also occurs at the onset of a vowel, usually stressed,
as in [ʔɑːp̥] *hop* (43), [ʔaːnʔ ʔaːɹɪəʔs] *Aunt Harriet's*
(49) (cf. Trudgill, 1974: 182; see also below under
Linking r). There are two instances of it as the
realization of /k/: [ɫɑɪʔ] *like* (2), [t'ɵʔ] *took* (72),
and one as the realization of /p/: [stɑʔt] *stopped*
(61).
There is a distinction of /ɵ/ and /ʌ/, no /h/,
no syllable-final /r/, and [ŋ] is not an underlying
phonological unit. Before vowels we find unstressed
final [i] as the realization of /ɨ/.

(a) *Lenition*. This process is not particularly widespread in E's speech, though there are number of
examples of stop → fricative, as in:

[tʃʌx əʔ] *chuck it* (18)

[ðass] *that's* (30)

[bɛ̝ːçən] *bacon* (39) and (40)

[-bɑ·dɨ xəd] *-body could* (54).

(Note that the example on line (30) has not undergone
Geminate Simplification.) Voicing of intervocalic
voiceless stops is even less common in E's, though a
number of Norwich speakers use it more often, e.g.

[pɒːdɨgəʔ] *Pottergate* (73).

[θɪŋg̊] *think* (68) is unusual; there is one instance
of a flap: [pɒɾ əʔ] *put it* (21).

(b) *Harmony*. The alveolars /t d n/ in particular
display place harmony, but in E's speech there are
many examples where it does not occur, e.g.

[oɵpm̩z] *opens* (4)

[ən̩ n̩ə] *and the* (5) and (14)

[sʌftʃ] *something* (7) and (47)

[ðæɪg gɨv] *they'd give* (12)

[ɪib bi] *he'd be* (23)

[dɨfɹəŋʔ kɫaːsəz] *different classes* (64)

116

[ad ðə] *had the* (14)

[ðɛɪdˀbɪn] *they'd been* (58)

[daün ðɛ̈] *down there* (52)

[ɪn̩ʔ gɑːʔ] *ain't got* (60).

/ð/-harmony also occurs, again with several exceptions, e.g.

[ən̩ n̩ə] *and the* (5) and (14)

[wɛ̈ ɫə] *well the* (11)

[ɔːɫ ɫə] *all the* (44) and (70)

[tˈɑɪm n̩ə] *time the* (52)

[lɛgz zə] *legs the* (55)

[ɪn ði] *in the* (25).

Voicing harmony occurs as well in [kos sæɪ] *course they* (39-40).
There is one instance of place harmony of /m/: [tˈɑɪŋ fə] *time for* (27). Nasalization of preceding vowels sometimes occurs: [kʌ̃nʔɹi] *country* (2), [ə̃m] *them* (12), [ə̃m͡n] *him* (23).
Palatal harmony is usual:

[mɒɪnd ʒüu] *mind you* (20)

[aʒ jü] *as you* (27)

[wəʒ jüʒəɫi] *was usually* (28)

[wɔnʃ jüud] *once you'd* (30)

[dɪd ʒə] *did you* (58).

(c) *CCS*. /t/ and /d/ are deleted in the usual circumstances, e.g.

[nɛks tüu] *next to* (11)

[ɹʌfəs pˈɫɛ̧ːs] *roughest place* (13)

[lɛf ʃʌɵɫdə] *left shoulder* (18)

[ɫɵ̀k daün] *looked down* (22)

[kˈʌɵɫ nɪ̀p] *cold nip* (28).

In one instance the / t / is retained where in most accents it is obligatory to delete it: [əɹʌ̀p̀ɛ̀ʃn] *eruption* (54), in contrast to [ɹ̲əfɫɛk̀ʃən]‾*reflection* (55).
The words *always* and *across* end in [st] before a vowel, but only [s] before a consonant, e.g.

117

[əkɹɔːst] (14), [ɔːɫwɪst] (16), [əkɹɔːs] (46), [ɔːɫəs] (51). Although this is epenthetic, historically speaking (cf. Strang, 1970: 166), the [t] can be treated as underlying in Norwich, subject to CCS as appropriate.

/n/ is sometimes deleted before /t/, realized as [ʔ], with no nasality of the vowel: [pˈɫɛʔi] *plenty* (47) (cf. Trudgill, 1974: 179).

Geminate Simplification occurs sporadically, e.g. [ɔːʃüu] (16), [wɛ̈ ɫə] (11).

(d) *UVD*. Unstressed vowels are often deleted under the same conditions as in the other localities, e.g.

[aü? ðæ?] *out of that* (23)

[ɛnɪ ði] *any of the* (34-35)

[ða? wz ʌɔnɪ] *that was only* (40)

[ɪi wz ʌɔni baü?] *he was only about* (42)

[bɪgɪ ən] *bigger than* (44).

There are also instances, less common elsewhere, such as:

[wɪivz] *weavers* (33)

[kˈæːbnə?] *cabinet* (56)

[aːfʔnɔn] *afternoon* (69).

Following a glottal stop, especially before another vowel, [ə] is deleted (cf. Stockport and Peasmarsh, above), e.g.

[baːðə ? aːsk] *bother to ask* (45)

[sʌftʃ ? ɪi?] *something to eat* (47).

In conjunction with linking r, this gives forms such as [goɔ ? ɹə] *go to a* (63). In [tɚːm] *to them* (3) the linking r and the two unstressed vowels have merged into a long r-coloured vocoid. This merging of [ə] with a preceding vowel is discussed in detail by Trudgill (1974: 159-62). It applies both within and across word boundaries. There are not many instances of this in E's speech, but [flɜː faˑɹə] *flew afire* (59) is one. When word-final /r/ is realized as [ə], this too affects a preceding vowel; thus, we find the following derivation: /küur/ ⇒ küuə ⇒ [kˈɜː] *cure* (68). In E's speech we can see that this merging does not always take place, e.g. [tˈü ə] *two or* (63).

As a final example of UVD I shall take the unstressed sequence *going to* (38), showing the interaction with other rules:

118

/goⱳən tüu/

Stress placement	⇒	goən tə
/t/-realization	⇒	goən ʔə
/n/-deletion	⇒	goə ʔə
UVD	⇒	[go ʔə].

(e) *Linking r.* As already mentioned in the Introduction, Norwich speakers extend the application of
linking r, e.g.

[tɚ:m] *to them* (3)

[ɪnʔəɹ ə] *into a* (7)

[dɹɔ:ɹən] *drawing* (24) and (66)

[bəɹ a:ʔ] *by heart* (32)

[tᵊɹ ɛnɪ] *to any* (34)

[goⱳ ʔ ɹə] *go to a* (63),

as₂well as in the expected environments, e.g. [wəɹ
æ:pɪ] *were happy* (8). Alongside these there are al̄so
a few instances of [ʔ] used as a link, e.g. [tə ʔa:p̂]
to hop (43).

(f) *Vowel lengthening.* It is necessary to differentiate those cases where vowel length is lexically
determined from those where it is determined by the
phonetic environment. On the one hand, words such
as *last* and *off* always have a long vowel and are
examples of the first type; on the other hand, *got*
and *that* are found with both long and short vowel
phases. In the latter category, stress plays an
important role, but the following sound may also
make it more likely that the vowel is lengthened.
In particular the voiceless stops (¹), the nasals
and /r/ seem to influence vowel length, though it is
also found before other sounds as well, e.g.

[nɑ:ɹɪdʒ] *Norwich* (5) and (37)

[ʃa:p̂] *shop* (7)

[æ:p̂ɪ] *happy* (8)

[æ:ŋɪn] *hanging* (16)

[pᶜa:ʔ] *pot* (23)

[wɒ:nʔ] *want* (25)

[bɑ:ðə] *bother* (45)

[sɑ:ŋ] *song* (51)

119

[kˈæːbnəʔ] *cabinet* (56)

[pɒːdɨgəʔ] *Pottergate* (73).

In one instance, [bɹɛ̝ːk̃fəst] (27), the vowel may be
the reflex of what was originally a long vowel anyway, even though it was shortened in most accents.
Without evidence in the form of alternative pronunciations with long and short vowel phases in this
speaker, it is difficult to determine to what extent
length is the result of a synchronic or a past
process. More data would be needed to come to any
firm conclusions regarding this somewhat complex
phenomenon in Norwich speech. It may also be that
there is a correlation between the last stressed
syllable in a breath group and this type of lengthening, except in the case of the high vowels /ɨ/ and
/ʊ/, though again there is insufficient evidence here
to come to any firm conclusions.

NOTES

([1]) It is interesting to note that this lengthening before voiceless sounds is opposite to what is
found in RP and some other accents (cf. Gimson, 1962:
90-91) and to what is normally interpreted as
"natural" (cf. Hyman, 1975: 172).

Chapter Seven

COMPARISON AND DISCUSSION

This chapter is a preliminary phonological statement
and interpretation of the data presented in the
individual localities. I hope to show the main
similarities and differences between the six accents
and indicate how these can be handled in terms of
rules. In the final section I shall indicate those
areas which, in the light of recent developments in
phonological theory, need further investigation.

THE MODEL CHOSEN
First of all, it is necessary to present the model of
description chosen. For the most part, I have followed Brown's (1972) scheme. Since I am not concerned
with morphological alternations, Brown's simpler model
(than, for example, Chomsky and Halle's) is more
suited to my purposes (cf. Brown's comments, 1972:
26-28). In particular, I want to argue in favour of
underlying elements specified only in terms of non-
redundant features and against the systematic
phonemic level. Lexical representations are concerned
with the distinctive features of the language in
question, the redundant ones being supplied by the
redundancy rules. Thus in English /f/ differs from
the other voiceless fricatives in that it is labial,
just as /p/ differs from the other voiceless stops.
The fact that the former is labiodental and the latter
bilabial is a matter of phonetic precision, not phonological contrasts: /f/ does not contrast with any
other voiceless labiodental consonant in English, nor
does /p/ contrast with any other voiceless bilabial.
(Contrast this with the fricatives of Ewe; Ladefoged,
1982: 144.) Furthermore, what is distinctive varies
from context to context. In English a nasal before
a stop will be homorganic with that stop, e.g.
[limp], [lint], [liŋk], so that place of articulation

is not a distinguishing feature of the nasals in
this position, since it is entirely dependent on the
following stop (¹). This has led some linguists to
establish an unspecified nasal /N/ in such cases in
English and other languages (cf. Fudge, 1969b;
Trudgill, 1974; Brown, 1972). The fully specified
systematic phonemic level may well equate to a body
of knowledge based partly on the spelling system,
which in English is morphophonemic in character, and
also related to a certain amount of taught, conscious
knowledge. That is to say, firstly, some of the
underlying forms incorporate morphophonemic infor-
mation, as often reflected in the spelling, which
has to be learnt more or less consciously and which
may not be available to all speakers to the same
degree. Secondly, especially as far as learned
vocabulary is concerned, knowledge of sets of related
words with alternating stem vowels and/or final
consonants is distributed very variously throughout
the native speakers of English (cf. also Cutler's,
1980, investigations referred to in the Introduction).
However, even in phonetic terms, the full specification of underlying segments may not be justified,
when consideration is given to language in the context
of its use. To quote Brown (1972: 46), a theory of
redundancy in the phonological component of a grammar
"must surely be to account, for instance, for the
perception of utterances which are masked by a high
degree of noise. The problem is one of identifying
the minimum input necessary for interpretation of an
utterance. It is a highly redundant theory of phonology which insists that a minimally redundant acoustic
input must always be processed (or indeed produced)
by stringing together fully specified systematic
phonemes and taking no account of the word, or message,
in which they appear.". Of course, the final sound
of *cat* and the initial sound of *tack* have to be
identified as the same, if this reflects the native
speaker's knowledge satisfactorily, but the resultant
/t/ does not have to be specified as:

    [- vocalic]
    [+ consonantal]
    [- high]
    [- back]
    [- low]
    [+ anterior]
    [+ coronal]
    [- voice]
    [- continuant]

[- nasal]
[- strident]

(or with any equivalent set of phonetic specifications) simply because it is pronounced that way in
initial position, or in some kind of standard,
careful speech. It is quite conceivable that many
native speakers of English never pronounce final
post-vocalic /t/ as anything but [ʔ].
In addition to Brown's arguments against the
systematic phonemic level (1972: 41-46), we may also
wish to argue that the unspecified nature of certain
features in the lexical entry forms reflects the
knowledge that native speakers have as to which
sounds harmonize and which do not. In the case of
the alveolars, so-called, the place of articulation
varies considerably, as we have already seen. We
can reflect this fact by leaving /t/, /d/ and /n/
unspecified for place and having process and realization rules to supply the appropriate feature.
Differentiation of place in the alveolar stops and
nasal may be more of a consciously learnt aspect of
the phonological system for some speakers of English,
in particular, those who use harmonized forms a great
deal (cf. Newton's (1970) and Ferguson's (1978)
comments on Modern Greek, a language which also
displays a lot of interword consonantal harmony in
colloquial speech)(²). It is interesting to note
that English, in many of its accents, shows what can
be interpreted as the first stage in final voiceless
stop loss found in a number of other languages (eg.
Thai, Mandarin, Maori). Voiceless stops harmonize
with following sounds, add a glottal closure, loose
the supraglottal closure, retaining only the glottal
one, and finally loose the closure altogether. (See
also Aitchison's discussion of this, 1981: 132-33.)
Such a change can be explained by progressive feature
loss in the underlying specifications (see below for
further discussion). In the English accents under
consideration (with the possible exception of Edinburgh, see Chapter 4 above) so far only the place
feature has disappeared from the underlying specification of the "alveolars".
The underlying (i.e. occurring in lexical entries)
stops and nasals in all the accents under consideration in this book have the following specifications,
using Ladefoged's system of feature classification
(1982: 254-66):

/p/	/t/	/k/	/b/
[-voice]	[-voice]	[-voice]	[+voice]
[stop]	[stop]	[stop]	[stop]
[labial]	[Øplace]	[velar]	[-nasal]
			[labial]

/d/	/g/	/m/	/n/
[+voice]	[+voice]	[Øvoice]	[Øvoice]
[stop]	[stop]	[stop]	[stop]
[-nasal]	[-nasal]	[+nasal]	[+nasal]
[Øplace]	[velar]	[labial]	[Øplace]

whereby Ø = unspecified, to be accounted for by a later rule. As mentioned above, in Edinburgh the informants use harmony less than in the other localities, so that it might be more appropriate for the feature [alveolar] to appear at this stage to mark the accent off as different in this respect. This would then make the harmony rule (see below) different for these informants. However, since more data would be needed before a more definite decision could be made on this point, I shall leave the underlying specifications the same for all the accents, thereby simplifying the statement of the harmony rule.

Redundancy rules, in the form of *if-then* conditions, account for the specification of [+voice] for the nasals and [-nasal] for the voiceless stops:

If	[+nasal]	If	[-voice]
	⇓		⇓
then	[+voice]	then	[-nasal]

The fricatives have the following specifications:

/f/	/θ/	/s/	/ʃ/
[-voice]	[-voice]	[-voice]	[-voice]
[fric]	[fric]	[fric]	[fric]
[labial]	[dental]	[alv]	[palatal]

/v/	/ð/	/z/	/ʒ/
[+voice]	[+voice]	[+voice]	[+voice]
[fric]	[Ømanner]	[fric]	[fric]
[labial]	[dental]	[alv]	[palatal]

The phonetic detail that /f/ and /v/ are realized as labiodental by most speakers is a matter of a redundancy rule of the form:

```
If    [fric]
      [labial]
         ⇓
then  [dental]
```

We may note that Y has an optional harmony rule
whereby [labial] sounds in her system may be bilabial
or labiodental depending on adjacent sounds, whether
stop or fricative (cf. Chapter 1 above). /ʃ/ and /ʒ/
have the feature [alv] added to their specifications
by redundancy rule. This gives all instances of [ʃ]
and [ʒ] the same phonetic specification whether underlying or a result of palatal harmony (cf. Lodge, 1981:
27-28).
The unspecified manner feature of /ð/ reflects
the widespread harmony to which this segment is
subject. In all the accents under consideration the
manner of articulation of /ð/ is determined by the
following sounds, as exemplified in the chapters
above.
The affricates /tʃ/ and /dʒ/ are members of the
stop series with the underlying place feature
[palatal] as with /ʃ/ and /ʒ/; a redundancy rule
accounts for the fricative release and the [alv]
specification. Palatal harmony of /t/ and /d/
involves copying the feature [palatal] to their
underlying specification with the same results (see
below for details).
/l/, /w/ and /j/ can be specified as follows:

```
  /l/         /w/         /j/

[approx]   [approx]   [approx]
[alv]      [labial]   [palatal]
```

The phonetic characteristics of /r/ are not the same
for each locality, though the rules which apply to
it may be (cf. Introduction, p. 13). Therefore, if
we wish to have the rules applicable to all accents
as appropriate, the specification of /r/ must be
sufficiently wide to cover the diverse realizations.
Since trills and approximants do not have many phonetic characteristics in common, we can resort to the
pseudo-phonetic feature [liquid] (cf. Ladefoged, 1982:
86) to reflect the phonological character of /r/, and
its behaviour in syllable structure along with /l/,
/j/ and /w/ (cf. Lass, 1976: 18). [liquid] could
then replace [approx] in the above specifications and
/r/ could be given an unspecified manner feature:

```
     /w/         /l/         /r/         /j/
[liquid]    [liquid]    [liquid]    [liquid]
[labial]    [alv]       [Ømanner]   [palatal]
```

The redundancy rules for /r/ would then be different
for each variant, depending on the realization
involved. Thus, speaker Y would have a rule:

```
If     [liquid]
       [Ømanner]
          ⇓
then   [approx]
       [labial]
       [dental]
```

whereas B would have:

```
If     [liquid]
       [Ømanner]
          ⇓
then   [approx]
       [retracted].
```

Some speakers have variant realizations of /r/, e.g.
G, H and E, for which variable rules may be necessary
(cf. Romaine's, 1978, treatment of /r/ in Edinburgh).

We should note in connection with Ø-specifications
of features that the redundancy rules have to be under-
stood in such a way that the feature specified Ø
disappears from the segment in question when the
redundant features are written in. This is because
within the Ladefoged system of classification the
features given Ø-specifications are hyponyms of the
redundant features; [place] and [manner] are not
features like [labial], [+voice], and [stop], but
are major class categories.

The vowels are rather more complicated than the
consonants, as there is much more variety in terms
of realization in the former. I shall not attempt a
full analysis of them here, but there are a few
aspects of the system which should be noted.

Lip-rounding, which is traditionally associated
with vowels (eg. Gimson, 1962), is not a distinctive
feature of the English vowel system; there are no
vowel contrasts carried solely by the opposition
rounded versus unrounded. It can be accounted for
by the redundancy rules. In Norwich it is associated
with certain consonants in some instances, so that
non-high back vowels, which are elsewhere unrounded,
take on lip-rounding after bilabial consonants (cf.

Chapter 6 above)(^{3}).

The main aspect of the vowel system I want to
consider is the status of length and the interpretation of diphthongs. In RP and some other accents
of English vowel length is not distinctive (cf.
Ladefoged, 1982: 84, 87 and 225). It is determined
by the voice characteristics of the following consonant, and in the context of an utterance the amount
of stress placed on a particular syllable affects the
length of the vowel. Of the accents presented here,
only Edinburgh has no length distinction (cf. Lass,
1976: 31); in fact, length is much more restricted
here than in RP. The other accents have contrastive
length, though the matter is not straightforward in
Norwich (see Chapter 6 above). The difference in
the occurrence of length in part accounts for the
rhythmic differences between the accents and may be
a matter of variant realizations of the same underlying units. The two questions to be answered are:
(i) Should the common underlying vowels be specified
as long or short? (ii) Are the diphthongs a separate
category?

Let us start with the second of these questions.
Traditional descriptions of RP (e.g. Gimson, 1962)
analyse the diphthongs as separate from the other
vowel phonemes, whereas descriptions of American
English by American linguists (e.g. Trager and Smith,
1951; Hockett, 1958; Chomsky and Halle, 1968) interpret them as vowel + glide; thus the vowel phase of
gate is /eɪ/ or /ey/ respectively (ignoring the more
complex SPE analysis for the moment). The vowels of
feet and *food* are also treated differently: /iː/ and
/uː/ on the one hand, and /iy/ and /uw/ on the other.
Lass (1976: 3-39) has argued at length for assigning
long vowels and diphthongs to the same phonological
class in English, namely vowel cluster (/VV/), the
difference between the two being "simply a matter of
identity or nonidentity of nuclear constituents"
(ibid.: 22). He dismisses the category glide in
English phonology as a misinterpretation of the
phonetic facts of the end point of the diphthongal
movements (ibid.: 15-19), as well as demonstrating
that the SPE feature of tenseness is nothing more
than a convenient abstraction (ibid.: esp. 39-50)(^{4}).
To these arguments he adds as further support that
such an analysis utilizing vowel clusters helps us to
give a simpler account of the historical process of
diphthongization of earlier long monophthongs (and,
incidentally, the less commonly discussed monophthong-
ization of earlier diphthongs, cf. ibid.: 32) than the

SPE account does, and enables us to give phonetically disparate accents the same dichotomous distinction in the vowels: /V/ versus /VV/. If we accept Lass's arguments (and his evidence is compelling), then the accents presented here, with the exception of Edinburgh, all have the /V/ - /VV/ distinction, whether or not /VV/ represents long monophthongs or diphthongs (⁵).

Given the /V/ - /VV/ distinction, we can now answer the first question as to the nature of the common underlying vowels. Historically, all accents of English appear to have had a long - short distinction in the vowels, and this is what is still preserved in the accents described here, with altered realizations. Table 1 gives the equivalences for the Middle English long vowels.

TABLE 1

ME	S	SB	P	C	N
i:	/aː/~/ae/	/ɑɪ/	/ɑɪ/	/ɔɪ/	/ɑɪ/
e:	/eɪ/	/ɪi/	/ɪi/	/ɪi/	/ɪi/
a:	/eː/~/ɛɪ/	/ɛɪ/	/ɛɪ/	/ɛɪ/	/ɛː/
u:	/æɒ/	/æɒ/	/æɒ/	/æɒ/	/ɑü/
o:	/ɪɒ/~/ou/	/ɒu/	/ɒu/	/ɒu/	/oɒ/*
ɔ:	/oː/~/ʌɒ/	/ʌɒ/	/ʌɒ/	/ʌɒ/	/üu/*

(The localities are represented by their initials.)

*The distribution of these sounds is somewhat complicated in Norwich, and involves /ɒ/ as well (cf. Trudgill, 1974: 72-73 and Trudgill and Foxcroft, 1978).

We can see from this that the /VV/ specification remains intact in each accent. If we take this as the basic form, accents such as Edinburgh will have to be subject to a shortening rule: $V_x V_x = V_x$, where x is a set of feature specifications.

The final point about the vowel system that I wish to make is the status of [ə] in the underlying representations. Where there are stress alternations, as in *photograph* - *photography*, [ə] is derivable from an appropriate full vowel by the stress placement rules. This would mean that in speaker Y's system the base morpheme *photograph*, for instance, would have the lexical entry form: /fʌʊtɑgraf/. On the other hand, where there are no stress alternations, as in *about*, the underlying representation will have

128

/ə/ as the initial vowel(⁶). In Table 4 below, none
of the accents under consideration has word-final /ə/
in words such as *carter*, *farmer*, etc., but those
forms of RP without any linking r do (cf. the Introduction above, p. 14).

COMPARISON
In the preceding section I have outlined what the
accents under discussion have in common. We must now
turn to a consideration of the differences between
the accents and formalize the process rules which
have been discussed above in the separate chapters.
In order to try to establish degrees of difference,
the following types of accent differentiation are
assumed: (1) variation in the number of phonological
contrasts, e.g. the vowels of *put* and *putt* distin-
guished or not; (2) variation in the incidence of the
phonological units in lexical items, e.g. *book* and
pool with the same or different vowels; (3) application of processes in different ways, e.g. *letter*
with intervocalic [s] or [d]; (4) phonetic realization differences, e.g. /r/ as [ʋ] or [ɹ], and
rhythmic differences related to syllable length;
(5) phonotactic differences, e.g. whether or not /r/
can occur before consonants; (6) differences in
articulatory setting, e.g. tense versus lax musculature. The different parts of the grammar involved
in pinpointing differences in accent reflect to some
extent the amount to which native speakers are
consciously aware of them. For example, people are
most conscious of the differences located in the
underlying segments, such as lack of the /ɒ/-/ʌ/
distinction and lack of /h/. Similarly, lexical
incidence and distributional differences (as in
Tables 3 and 4 below) tend to be recognized, since
they too involve segments and their arrangement. On
the other hand, phonetic differences, which involve
only one or two features, or a redundancy rule, are
less likely to be consciously picked out, and
processes such as harmony are very often totally
ignored.
    Table 2 is a comparison of the systematic
differences displayed by the informants under
consideration in this book, as far as the vowels
are concerned. (The localities are indicated by
initial.)

TABLE 2

	S	SB	P	E	C	N
	/εe/ ⎫	/εɪ/	/εɪ/	/e/	/εɪ/	⎧ /æɪ/
	/e:/ ⎭					⎩ /ε̣:/
	/o:/	/ʌɵ/	/ʌɵ/	/o/	/ʌɵ/	⎧ /ʌɵ/
						⎨ /oɵ/
	/ʉu/	/ɵu/	/ɵu/	⎫ /u/	/ɵu/	⎨ /üu/
	/o/ ⎰	/ɵ/	/ɵ/	⎭	⎰ /ɵ/	/ɵ/
	⎱ /ʌ/	/ʌ/	/ʌ/	⎭ /ʌ/		/ʌ/

NB: The /εe/:/e:/ distinction does not apply to
speaker Y, who also has a diphthong /ʌɵ/ rather than
/o:/, and /ɪɵ/ rather than /ʉu/. Norwich /æɪ/ is
not the equivalent of Stockport /εe/, having a
different historical origin.

The distinctions found only in one or two accents,
indicated by braced pairs in Table 2, show the extent
to which the underlying vowel systems differ at this
fundamental level. In other respects the systems of
the accents under discussion are the same, as far as
the underlying units are concerned.
    Table 3 gives examples of differences in
lexical incidence.

TABLE 3

	S	SB	P	E	C	N
last	/a/	/ɑ:/	/a:/	/a:/	/a/~/a:/	/a:/
book	/ʉu/(N)	/ɵ/	/ɵ/	/u/	/ɵ/	/ɵ/
boat	/o:/(N)	/ʌɵ/	/ʌɵ/	/o/	/ʌɵ/	/ɵ/
cart	/a:/	/ɑ:/	/ar/	/ar/	/a:/	/a:/
serve	/ø:/	/ə:/	/ɵr/	/εr/	/ɵ:/	/ɐ:/~/ɜ:/
church	/ø:/	/ə:/	/ɵr/	/ʌr/	/ɵ:/	/ɐ/
more	/oə/(N)	/ɔ:/	/ɔr/	/or/	/ɔ:/	/ɔ:/
	/ɔ:/(Y)					
sort	/ɔ:/	/ɔ:/	/ɔr/	/ɔr/	/ɔ:/	/ɔ:/
tall	/ɔ:/	/ɔ:/	/ɔ:/	/ɔ/	/ɔ:/	/ɔ:/

NB: Speaker Y often uses an unrounded form of /ɔ:/.

The consonantal systems are less varied, but we have noted that /h/ is usually not an underlying unit. /ng/ is realized differently in different accents, but this is a matter of rule variation (see below). Similarly, /r/ may occur post-vocalically before a consonant or it may be restricted from occurring in that position, as described in the Introduction (pp. 12-14); this is a matter of lexical incidence. Table 4 gives a number of underlying forms for words involving historical /r/.

TABLE 4

	S̲	S̲B̲	P̲	E̲	C̲	N̲
car	/kaːr/	/kɑːr/	/kar/	/kar/	/kaːr/	/kaːr/
cart	/kaːt/	/kɑːt/	/kart/	/kart/	/kaːt/	/kaːt/
carter	/kaːtr̩/	/kɑːtr̩/	/kartr̩/	/kartr̩/	/kaːtr̩/	/kaːtr̩/

THE PROCESS RULES
I now want to consider the rules for handling the phonological processes discussed in the individual chapters and compare their application across the six accents. I shall start with the stops and consider harmony and glottal reinforcement. The following redundancy rules account for the harmony of /t/, /d/ and /n/, and their specification as [alveolar] elsewhere.

1. If   [stop]
        [Øplace]
          ⇓
   then [αplace]/ _____   C
                          [αplace]

2. If   [stop]
        [Øplace]
          ⇓
   then [alv]

The rules cannot be collapsed because 1 is optional and 2 obligatory, and 2 must apply even in the context specified in 1, if the latter does not apply. The rules have to account for the fact that /d/ in *good man* can be realised as [b] or [d], whilst in *good evening* it must be [d]. (See also footnote 10 of this chapter.)

Glottal reinforcement involves a change in

phonation type (cf. Ladefoged, 1982: 258). In
English the basic distinction is between those sounds
that have voice and those that do not. The third
possibility - simultaneous glottal stop - is a
derived (i.e. not basic) articulation of the voiceless
series in certain contexts. (The glottal stop is
neither voiced nor voiceless because of the position
of the vocal cords; it is, however, 'without voice'.)
Rule 3 accounts for glottal reinforcement.

3. [-voice] ⇒ [glottal]/ _____ $ (opt.)
                         [stop]

The context specifies syllable-final position. In
most accents this occurs before another consonant or
a pause, not before a vowel. This is because a
following vowel requires syllable overlap, that is
the segment in question is ambisyllabic, whether
underlying or derived by concatenation in the speech
chain([7]). Thus, *city* and *got a* have the following
syllable structure, using a dependency notation (see
Anderson, ms):

Glottal reinforcement cannot apply in cases of overlap as indicated by the environment template, where
the syllable boundary follows the stop segment.
However, in Norwich we do find intervocalic reinforced
stops, so that only in word-initial position are they
ruled out. We, therefore, need to posit a different
underlying syllable structure for words like *city* for
those speakers who always have glottally reinforced
stops (or glottal realization of /t/, see below).
This means no overlapping, and resyllabification via
concatenation does not take place either, i.e.

 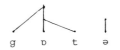

If there are alternating forms with and without
glottal reinforcement, then we need a rule of resyllabification under certain circumstances. I shall
discuss this further below, when I consider variation
in glottal realization of /t/. (See also footnote 8
of this chapter.)

We now have to account for the occurrence of [ʔ] only as the realization of /t/. Rule 4 has slightly different contexts for its operation as shown below. Table 5 indicates how these alternative versions of the rule are distributed in my informants' speech.

4. [-voice] ⇒ [glottal]/ _____ (C)$ (opt.)
    [Øplace]   [+voice][stop]

as in *hit, went, cotton, Scotland, got a,* but not
**first, *loft, *centre, *bottle, *petrol, *better, *ten.* The difference between *cotton* with [ʔ] and
bottle, petrol with [t] is one of syllabification.
In the former instance underlying /t/ must be
syllable-final, whereas in the latter examples the
/t/ is ambisyllabic and therefore does not fit the
environment template. Intervocalic /t/ is also
excluded from the environment specification in that
it, too, is ambisyllabic.

4'.   / _____ (C)$ C
        [+voice][stop]

The inclusion of the rightmost C excludes examples
such as *got a* from glottal realization.

4''.   / _____ (C)$
        [stop]

4'' allows words with a voiceless sound before /t/,
e.g. *afternoon, lost* to be subject to the rule. In
each case rule 4 is subject to the condition that the
stress immediately following /t/ is not greater than
the stress immediately preceding it (cf. Leslie, ms).

In cases where /k/ is realized as [ʔ] we need
rule 5.

5. [-voice] ⇒ [glottal]/ V _____ (#)C
    [velar]   [stop]

as in *picture, took me* but not **kicker, *took it,
think. I shall return to a consideration of glottal
reinforcement and glottal realization below, when I
discuss lenition and related processes.
    The above rules do not allow glottal reinforce-
ment of word-initial /t/ and /k/ or glottal realization, but we must note the following examples:

[spoːs ʔ beɪ] *supposed to be* Stockport (75)

[jɒu k̩̍ŋ] *you can* Peasmarsh (26)

[ʌp ? sɪi] *up to see* Peasmarsh (43)

[jʊ k̚ŋ̩] *you can* Coventry (58)

[daün ?ə] *down to* Norwich (34)

[bɑːðə ? aːsk] *bother to ask* Norwich (45).

In such cases the syllable structure has been changed
by unstressed vowel reduction or deletion, so that
the /t/ and /k/ take up syllable positions where they
can be realized as [?]. In cases such as *you can* and
down to the initial /k/ and /t/ belong to both
syllables:

 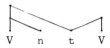

If the stops retain their ambisyllabicity, they are
realized as oral stops. If, however, they become
the final consonants of the first syllable and become
detached from the second one, they are realized as
[?]. The same process accounts for H's alternations
of [t] and [?] in words like *centre*:

In some instances the operation of UVD produces the
same end of syllable positions, eg.

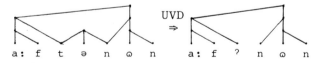

This is a Norwich pronunciation (line 69); I have
not included the detail of /aː/. If there is no
alternation between [t] and [?], but the surface form
is always [?], then the underlying form must have a
syllable-final /t/ not an ambisyllabic one([8]), as
suggested above in relation to glottal reinforcement
in Norwich.

This brings us to the examples involving the
infinitive particle *to* (*to*-inf) and, in Stockport
only, the definite article. In Norwich a form such
as [jüs ?ə] (57) is accounted for by rule 4'' after
the syllable structure has been altered, because

there is no reference to the voice characteristics of the preceding environment. However, this is not the case with 4 and 4', where voiceless sounds are excluded from the environment template. Therefore, *supposed to be* and *up to see* in the above examples should be excluded from glottal realization according to the rule. In those accents that allow glottal realization in such cases it is only with *to*-inf, not prepositional *to*. Thus, *supposed to be* above is well-formed, whereas

$$*[\text{klo:s ? bɛɹe}] \ close \ to \ Bury$$

is not. In Stockport we can add the glottal realiz-ation of *the* to these examples, as the only other morpheme involved in such environments, e.g.

$$[\text{pas ? saɫt}] \ pass \ the \ salt,$$

but not $$*[\text{pas? ə beske?}] \ passed \ a \ biscuit.$$

In Chapter 1 I suggested a possible treatment for the glottal realization of *the*, which can be revised in the light of the preceding discussion of glottal realization. *The* and *to*-inf are exceptions and will have to be treated so. One way to do this would be to have a 'dummy' underlying preceding [+voice] in the lexical entry for these two words; thus:

$$/_{[+\text{voice}]}\text{tV}/ \quad to\text{-inf}$$

$$/_{[+\text{voice}]}\text{ðV}/ \quad the$$

(where the exact specification of V is irrelevant). The dummy voice specification would then have to be deleted, as follows:

6. $[+\text{voice}] \Rightarrow \emptyset \ / \ [-\text{voice}]\_\_\_\_[\text{glottal}] \ (\text{obl.})$

This gives the following derivations:

	$/\text{pas}_{[+\text{voice}]}\text{ðV salt}/$	$/\text{ʌp}_{[+\text{voice}]}\text{tV sɪi}/$
Stress placement	$\Rightarrow \text{pas}_{[+\text{voi}]}\text{ðə salt}$	$\text{ʌp}_{[+\text{voi}]}\text{tə sɪi}$
t-insertion	$\Rightarrow \text{pas}_{[+\text{voi}]}\text{tðə salt}$	____
UVD	$\Rightarrow \text{pas}_{[+\text{voi}]}\text{tð salt}$	$\text{ʌp}_{[+\text{voi}]}\text{t sɪi}$
ð-deletion	$\Rightarrow \text{pas}_{[+\text{voi}]}\text{t salt}$	____
4	$\Rightarrow \text{pas}_{[+\text{voi}]}\text{? salt}$	$\text{ʌp}_{[+\text{voi}]}\text{? sɪi}$

6 ⇒ [pas ? saɫt]   [ʌp ? sɪi]

Even the absolute initial instances could be accounted for in this way, if we alter the environment of rule 6 to include a pause (∅):

6. [+voice] ⇒ ∅ / $\begin{cases} [-\text{voice}] \\ ∅ \end{cases}$ ____[glottal](obl.).

Table 5 gives a comparison of rule application for the voiceless stops.

TABLE 5

S	SB	P	E	C	N
1	1	1	1	1	1
2	2	2	2	2	2
3	3	3	3	3	3
4(Y) 4'(N)	4	4'	4	4'	4''
5(Y)	5	6	5(H)		5
6(N)					

In Norwich rule 6 is unnecessary, because the context is covered by the extended template of 4'', as mentioned above. The differences in glottal realization distribution are determined by what we may refer to as the operation of Right Release (RR), that is the loss of a right subjunction by an ambisyllabic /t/, as described above. In Norwich and speaker H in Edinburgh RR is applied far more frequently than in the other informants, e.g. *city* is usually:

Y uses it very occasionally, as in [bɛ?ə] (41). Speaker N occasionally uses rule 4, as in [ɡɑ?] + V (84), rather than 4'. In formal terms this means that the environment template of 4' loses its rightmost C.

We can now turn to a consideration of CCS and some other instances of deletion. CCS can be given as rule 7:

7. [αvoice] ⇒ ∅ / C ____ +C (opt.)
   [stop]   [αvoice]
   [-nasal]

where + is a morpheme boundary. This deletes a stop,
mostly /t/ and /d/, in the appropriate environment.
Similarly, /k/ is deleted in /-sk+/ sequences, and
in those accents where /ng/ is realized as [ŋg] /g/
also deletes, as in [θeŋz], Stockport (36). The
specification [-nasal] excludes /-lm/ and /-ln/
sequences from the rule(9). In Edinburgh /r/ must
be excluded from the preceding context, since the
/d/ in *word*, for example, does not delete before a
consonant. In this respect /r/ acts differently
from its fellow liquid /l/, and can even precede /l/
to produce three-consonant clusters not permitted
in non-rhotic accents; words such as *world, words*
are not subject to CCS.

/n/ is different from the non-nasal stops and
must be dealt with by separate rules, even though
in the individual localities I included it under CCS.
In some accents a word like *want* may have any of the
following pronunciations (with the appropriate vowel
quality, which is irrelevant to the present point):
[want], [wãnt], [wanˀ], [wãnˀ], [waˀ], [wãˀ], though
they do not all occur in all the accents under
discussion here. To account for all these forms we
need the optional rules 8 and 9.

8.　　V　　⇒　　V　　/ ___ C　　　(opt.)
　　　[+nasal]　[+nasal]

9. [stop]　⇒　　∅　　/ V___ˀ#　　(opt.)
　 [+nasal]

These give us the following possible derivations
each stage of which is a possible pronunciation:

		/want/			/want/
8	⇒	[wãnt]	4	⇒	[wanˀ]
4	⇒	[wãnˀ]	9	⇒	[waˀ]
9	⇒	[wãˀ]			

None of the accents presented here allow 9 to apply
before [t]. In Edinburgh neither speaker has rules
8 and 9, and only H has rule 6. Neither of the
Peasmarsh informants has rules 8 and 9 either. In
Stockport speaker Y extends the context of rule 9
to include alveolar fricatives and a pause, e.g.
[ẽ st-] (10), [t'∅ĩz] (11), [ðɛ̃] (7). In [ə̃ m-] (34),
as in [wɛ̃ m-] Coventry (68), Place Harmony and
Geminate Simplification have been applied (cf. p.106
above). In Shepherd's Bush too, speaker C has
extended the context to both alveolar and dental
fricatives, e.g. [maĩz] (5), [ʊ̃ ðə] (28), [sã̃θɪŋk̃](48).

137

There are also examples in her speech of rule 9 being applied to [ʔ] = /k/, e.g. [θiʔ?] (5) and (9).

I have already discussed /g/-deletion in Chapters 1 and 2 above to account for [ŋ] without a following velar stop, but in fact it is less straightforward than just a simple deletion rule. The rules involved apply in other environments in some of the accents under discussion. First we need a rule for left-to-right voicing harmony, as in [wɛnt] ⇒ [wɛnd]:

10. [-voice] ⇒ [+voice] / [+nasal] _____ #
$$\left[\text{stop}\right]$$

(This may be seen as an instance of lenition.) Then we need a rule for left-to-right nasal harmony, as in [wɛnd] ⇒ [wɛnn]:

11. [-nasal] ⇒ [+nasal] / [+nasal] _____ #
$$\begin{bmatrix}\text{+voice}\\\text{stop}\end{bmatrix}$$

These two rules would also apply to the sequence /ng/, so we have the following derivations:

		/went/	/send/	/sɪng/
1	⇒	went	send	sɪŋg
10	⇒	wend	——	——
11	⇒	wenn	senn	sɪŋŋ

Geminate Simplification, rule 12, can now be applied to the outputs of rule 11.

12. C_i ⇒ Ø / C_i_____ (opt.)

where i is a set of feature specifications.

12 ⇒ [wen] [sen] [sɪŋ]

At this point we may note that some of the rules are optional in some circumstances and obligatory in others, even in the same accent([10]). For example, *went* and *send* can have any of the stages shown in the derivation above as surface forms in Shepherd's Bush, but only the output of rules 11 and 12 in Peasmarsh, which means that in the latter locality rule 11 is obligatory, if rule 10 is chosen([11]). On the other hand, /sɪng/ is subject to all three rules in all the accents except Stockport. It is true that historical changes can be handled quite satis- factorily in terms of rules spreading, retreating or

138

being lost altogether. In the case under discussion /-mb/ has been eliminated from English by these rules, /-ng/ not quite, because of the alternations such as *long - longer*, and /-nd/ is least affected. However, there are other considerations from a synchronic point of view. The difference between optional and obligatory application of rules in this particular case may indicate that we should postulate an underlying /ŋ/ in words like *sing* which have no morphological alternations([12]).

If we take /ng/ as the underlying form of [ŋ], we can explain the different pronunciations of *length* with final [-ŋθ] or [-n̥θ], which varies from person to person rather than locality to locality. These forms can be accounted for in terms of different ordering in the application of rules 1 and 7, giving the following derivations:

		/leng+θ/				/leng+θ/
1	⇒	leŋg+θ	7	⇒	len+θ
7	⇒	[leŋθ]	1	⇒	[len̥θ]

(I am not concerned with the removal of the morpheme boundary.)

Table 6 presents the distribution of rules 7-12 in the six localities. Where rules 10, 11 and 12 are used only in the case of [ŋ], I have put an asterisk.

TABLE 6

S	SB	P	E	C	N
7	7	7	7(H)	7	7
8	8	10	10*	8	8
9(N) 9'(Y)	9''	11	11*	9	9
12	10	12	12*	10	10*
	11			11	11*
	12			12	12

Palatal harmony of /t/ and /d/ can be accounted for by rule 1 and the redundancy rules mentioned above which add [alv] and fricative release to palatal stops. Rule 13 accounts for palatal harmony in the case of /s/ and /z/.

13. [alv]   (opt.)
    [fric]
     ⇓
    [palatal] / ____ [palatal]

Some speakers block rule 13 and rule 1 from operating on /s/ and /z/, when [t] or [d] intervenes, i.e. *last chair* with CCS is [las tʃɛ:] not [laʃ tʃɛ:] (with different vowels as appropriate), and *Stuart* begins with [stʃ-] not [ʃtʃ-]. No speakers allow palatal harmony to apply to /t/ and /d/ before /tʃ/ or /dʒ/, thus *hot cheese* does not have [-tʃ tʃ-], and *glazed jars* does not have [-dʒ dʒ-]. After palatal harmony has occurred, the conditioning /j/ may be deleted if an unstressed vowel follows, as given in rule 14.

14. [liquid] ⇒ ∅ / ____ V̌
    [palatal]   [palatal]

The derivation below is that of [kaʃə̆], Stockport (26).

```
        /kasts jV̌/
 7   ⇒   -ss j-
13   ⇒   -ʃʃ j-
12   ⇒   -ʃ j-
14   ⇒   [-ʃ]
```

There are cases where both rule 13 and CCS are involved and the latter is obligatory. For example, in *correction* CCS is obligatory, but not in *correct them*. It is not the intervening morpheme boundary that requires CCS, since in *lifts* and *costs*, for example, the /t/ can be retained. It is, rather, the combination of the palatal and the morpheme boundary that is crucial. We could, therefore, revise rule 7 as follows, giving one obligatory context and one optional one:

7. [αvoice] ⇒ ∅ / ____   { [palatal]⁺ } (obl.)
    [stop]   [αvoice] {   }
    [-nasal]   {   + C   } (opt.)

The morpheme boundary appears after the palatal consonant in the environment template to allow the rule to apply optionally to palatals derived by rule 13, as in *costs you* above (ie. *cost+s*). This means that the derivation of *correction* is as follows:

```
        /kərekt+jən/
 1   ⇒   -ktʃ+j-
14   ⇒   -ktʃ+-
 7   ⇒   [-kʃ-]
```

Rule 14 is also obligatory in this context.

We must now return to /ð/, which I have dealt
with under the general heading ð-harmony. /ð/ was
given an unspecified manner feature above, because
it is realized in a variety of ways, as we have seen
in the individual chapters. In fact, we are dealing
with two rules, plus rules 1 and 11. The redundancy
rule 15 accounts for the contextual variants.

15. If   [Ømanner]
          [dental]
                ⇓
   then   [αmanner] / [αmanner] ____   (opt.)
                       [alv]
                       ⇓
   otherwise   [fric]

In the case of /-n ð-/ we have the following derivation:

        /n ð/
1   ⇒   n̪ ð
15 ⇒   n̪ d̪
11 ⇒   n̪ n̪

in which all stages are possible surface versions.
The output of rule 15 is more common in Coventry
than in the other localities. In the case of /-l ð-/,
/-z ð-/, /-s ð-/, /-(d)ʒ ð-/ and /-(t)ʃ ð-/, there
is an optional change of [dental] to [alv], as in
rule 16([13]).

16. [dental] ⇒ [alv] / ([fric]   )   (opt.)
                        ([liquid]) ([fric]   )
                        [alv]   ([liquid])

Thus:

        /l ð/   /z ð/   /tʃ ð/
15 ⇒   l l̪   z ð   tʃ ð
16 ⇒   l l   z z   tʃ z

(The first instance of [l] would, of course, be
velarized.)

LENITION AND SYLLABLE STRUCTURE
As a final section to this chapter, I would like to
take up some issues which point towards a non-linear
approach to phonology, to which I have already
alluded above in relation to glottal realization.
In so doing, I hope to pick out areas for more

141

detailed investigation in the future.

In the Introduction I referred to a general schema for lenition as presented by Anderson and Ewen (1980: 28) and expanded by Ewen (1980: 175). Such phenomena as lenition are used by supporters of natural process phonology to argue against the SPE feature system which does not allow "strength scales" to be captured as unitary. Within the dependency framework proposed by Anderson and Ewen (1980) and Ewen (1980), lenition is seen as a gradual increase in the dominance and preponderance of the element $|V|$ (= "relatively periodic") as opposed to $|C|$ (which "correlates with the presence of zeros in the acoustic record of that segment") (cf. Anderson and Ewen, 1980: 25). These are components of the categorial gesture, the part of the phonological representation concerned with consonantality, voice, continuancy and sonorance (cf. Ewen, 1980: 134). Sequences of segment change in the history of various languages, such as:

$$x \longrightarrow \gamma \longrightarrow w \longrightarrow \emptyset$$

$$p \longrightarrow b \longrightarrow \beta$$

occurring in intervocalic position, are used as evidence for the establishment of such processes as natural and universal. (Child language acquisition phenomena are also cited as supportive evidence, e.g. Stampe, 1979, but see also Aitchison's caveat, 1981: 180-83.) However, there are other paths to deletion than the one exemplified above, and I would like to mention two here, one of which is particularly relevant to my data and does not seem at first sight to be related to lenition.

Both voiceless stops and voiceless fricatives disappear in circumstances other than intervocalically([14]), e.g.

Old Chinese γiep > Mandarin çiε;
compare Latin *septem* with Greek *hepta* > Modern Greek [εfta];
Latin *fumus* > Spanish *umo*.

We can see similar changes in English, both synchronically and diachronically, either in part or in toto. Consider glottal reinforcement in syllable-final position and the [ʔ] allophone of /t/ and /k/. Similarly, the voiceless velar fricative has disappeared from the English phoneme inventory:

εçtə > εɪçt > εɪht > εɪt

dɔxtər > dɔɷxtər > dɔɷhtər > dɔɷtər

(For a discussion of this process in more detail, see Lodge, ms.)

On the basis of this and similar evidence we can represent the deletion paths informally as follows:

p, t, k $\longrightarrow$ p̃, t̃, k̃ $\longrightarrow$ ʔ $\longrightarrow$ ∅

f, s, θ, x $\longrightarrow$ h $\longrightarrow$ ∅

In both cases the process involves the loss of supra-glottal stricture before the segment disappears altogether. The phase before deletion is simply [stop] and [-voice], respectively (cf. Lass, 1976: 163).

If we interpret this progression in terms of the activity of the vocal cords, we can see that all three types of deletion involve this aspect of articulation. In lenition we are dealing with vibrating vocal cords, with the stops with closed vocal cords, and with the fricatives with open vocal cords. If these are isolated separately as elements in the categorial gesture: |V|, |ʔ| and |O|, respectively, in a dependency notation, then we can explain the processes involved as loss of all the other phonological features before final deletion. (See Ewen, 1980, Lodge, 1981, and Davenport and Staun, ms, for arguments relating to the constituents in the categorial gesture.) Terms like "lenition" and "weakening" are not suitable for describing all three types of deletion path, especially as glottal reinforcement appears to be a "strengthening" of articulation, so I shall suggest the more general term "progressive feature loss" to cover all three.

We should perhaps enquire why some sounds seem to be subject to apparent strengthening processes when they are in an inherently weak syllable position. The notion of relatively strong and weak positions in the syllable has been developed by a number of phono-logists (eg. Hooper, 1976, Foley, 1977, Liberman and Prince, 1977, Kiparsky, 1979, Selkirk, 1980, and Ewen, 1980) as an inherent property of phonological structure at various levels. Such strength hier-archies are related to sonority, the most sonorous sound being the strongest. In metrical phonology and dependency phonology the English word *pad* would be given the following syllable structures respectively:

$$\begin{array}{ccc} & \sigma & \\ & \diagup\diagdown & \\ w & \diagup s & \diagdown w \\ | & \diagup\diagdown & | \\ p & a & d \end{array} \qquad \begin{array}{ccc} & & \\ & \diagup|\diagdown & \\ p & a & d \end{array}$$

(cf. Kiparsky, 1979, and Anderson, ms.) In the
dependency tree strength can be read off in terms of
the nodes and the degrees of dependency([15]). In
both representations syllable-initial position is
weaker than nuclear position, but stronger than
syllable-final position. In other accounts of
syllable strength (eg. Hooper, 1976, and Foley, 1977)
we find that syllable-initial position is character-
ised as strong. However, with the more subtle,
relative strengths proposed by both metrical and
dependency phonology, we can explain why weakening
to zero is less common in initial position than in
final position because the former is relatively
stronger. If we accept the notion of relative
strengths within the syllable, we can postulate
processes which attempt to balance out the syllable
values as well as reinforcing them([16]). That is why
we find glottal reinforcement in English, an attempt
to strengthen a weak syllable position. English is
in a "strengthening phase" in this respect, in that
it has glottal reinforcement in most accents, although
there are signs of weakening in some accents, including those presented in this study, in that /p t k/
tend to be realized as [ʔ], the order of frequency
being /t/, then /k/, then /p/ least often. Mandarin,
on the other hand, has weakened the final stops to
zero.

Another instance of strengthening a weak
syllable position is devoicing of final voiced
obstruents, complete in German and Russian, for
instance, but only partial in English. We can find
the alternation of strengthening and weakening in
West Yorkshire voicing harmony (cf. Wells, 1982: 367,
and Leslie, ms) in a word like *Bradford*, where /d/
being in syllable-final position is weaker than /f/
in the initial position of the following syllable.
We can represent this informally, as follows:

where $\overline{\leftarrow}$ = "strengthens to", and $\overline{\rightarrow}$ = "weakens to".

In order to incorporate these aspects of
lenition into our rules, we may wish to relate more
closely rules which have so far been presented as
separate. Let us take CCS and glottal reinforcement.
The rules given above, 3 and 7, are quite distinct
from one another. However, when we consider some of
the sounds affected by them, namely /t/ and /k/, we
could postulate the following progression as the
deletion path related to glottal closure, as
described above.

(i)   Add glottal closure to all voiceless
stops in context X.
(ii)   Remove supraglottal closure from all
glottally reinforced stops in context Y.
(iii) Remove glottal stop in context Z.

The first stage of the progression is captured by
rule 3; the second and third stages by rules 4, 5 and
7. On the other hand, we can present stages (ii) and
(iii) somewhat differently in rules 17 and 18.

17. [place] $\Rightarrow \emptyset$ / _____ (opt.)
    [glottal]
    [stop]

18. [glottal] $\Rightarrow \emptyset$ / _____ + C (obl.)
    [stop]   [-voice]

If rule 17 is chosen, rule 18 must be applied, since
in the accents presented here with the exception of
Norwich, forms such as *[pʌɒsʔmən] *postman* are not
well-formed, whereas forms such as [sɔ:ɬʔmaɪn] *salt
mine* are. This progression means that each glottal
realization is generated via glottal reinforcement,
and each deletion via both glottal reinforcement and
glottal realization. The disadvantages of this
approach are twofold: the glottal realization of
/p t k/ has already been noted as being different in
frequency for each of the stops, and this can only
be accounted for by the optionality of rule 17; the
deletion of /d/ under the same circumstances as /t/
has to be accounted for by a separate rule. It is,
of course, true that in the case of /d/-deletion as
determined by CCS, there is no evidence in the data
presented here that we are dealing with a gradual
deletion path, i.e. there are no instances of intermediate stages suggesting a path such as d ⟶ z ⟶
ȷ ⟶ $\emptyset$. We, therefore, have to assume a "direct"
deletion: d ⟶ $\emptyset$.
    In the case of speaker Y /n/ displays the whole

145

range of a lenition path to deletion; the following
are all realizations of /n/: [n], [ɨ̃], [ʊ̃], [j̃], [w̃],
[ə̃], [ʌõ̃], [øĩ̃], Ø, the last two phonetic realizations
being nasalization of part of the preceding vowel
phase. These all occur in weak syllable position
and the non-nasal features are determined by the
following sound(s), i.e. [ɨ̃] occurs before /l/, [w̃]
before ([ʔ])/w/, and so on([17]).
   I have not gone into any detail regarding
syllable structure, but have referred to the syllable
throughout both informally and in the rules, e.g.
rule 3. I have taken the view, supported by both
metrical and dependency phonology, that the syllable
is an appropriate level of phonological abstraction
for the statement of certain regularities. Rule 3,
for instance, would be more complicated without
reference to the syllable boundary. We also have to
refer to syllabification to account for the difference in the realization of /t/ in Stockport *cotton*
versus *bottle*, for example. Furthermore, if we
accept the notion of differential strength distributed
in the syllable, some of the process rules can be
formulated in terms of strength/weakness. We can
explain why CCS operates in the way it does. Three
consecutive weak positions reduce to two and it is
the weakest position that is lost, e.g.

In the last stage there is resyllabification to
produce overlap. On the other hand, in a CCV sequence
the final weak C is strengthened by resyllabification
making it ambisyllabic:

   If such strength scales can be shown to be
universal to natural languages, then considerable
savings can be made in the grammars of individual
languages. Their language-specific relevance is
easier to demonstrate and it may well be that all the
processes discussed in this study can be related to
syllable structure and relative strength. That has
yet to be demonstrated.

NOTES

[1]. Stampe's (1979: 32) point that where no alternation occurs [m] is different from [ŋ] in that the former is underlying but the latter is not, may be valid on psychological grounds, but he offers no support for his argument other than the spelling.

[2]. Further investigation of how children acquire their accents might give some indication as to what feature specifications are minimally necessary for the identification of utterances in that particular accent. It is quite clear, even on the basis of a small amount of evidence, that harmonized forms are learnt early, so that harmony, at least, constitutes an important part of the phonological system for the child as well as for the adult (cf. Lodge, 1983). Of course, Stampe (1979) would argue that all the child has to do is learn where to suppress such natural processes as harmony.

[3]. More investigation of lip-rounding in consonants is necessary to give a proper statement of this (cf. Brown's, 1981, discussion).

[4]. In the descriptions of the general phonetic characteristics of each accent I have used the terms *tense* and *lax* with reference to the musculature of the speech organs; these are not to be associated with the SPE features [+tense], [-tense].

[5]. Historically speaking, the modern English diphthongs come from different sources, either long vowels, as in *name*, or vowel + consonant, as in *day*. Although none of the accents presented here have this feature, several Northern accents still differentiate some instances of original long vowel and original vowel + consonant, as in *bite* with [aɪ] and *night* with [ɪi] (cf. Lodge, 1973). It may be that such a distinction should be made in the underlying segments of even RP, especially if we wish to account for the morphological alternations *right - righteous*, as opposed to *delight - delicious* (where the spelling of the noun is misleading), in the phonological component (see Lodge, ms).

[6]. I do not propose to offer any further support for such an analysis beyond the alternation criterion. However, there is some evidence from mis-spellings of unstressed vowels by both children and adults to suggest that we are not justified in assuming full vowels for all surface instances of [ə], since such an assumption is arbitrarily based on the standard orthography.

[7]. For arguments concerning syllable overlap and ambisyllabicity, see Anderson and Jones (1977: 94-112) and Ewen (1980: 180-84).

147

[8] In Leslie's discussion of glottal allophony (ms) he gives the rule of resyllabification as Left Capture, that is the segment in question loses its attachment to the underlying syllable to the right and is then "captured" by the syllable to the left. However, if the /t/ is made ambisyllabic in the underlying representation, the rule is one of releasing the right-hand dependency (Right Release), leaving only the left-hand one, as shown in the representations of *centre* above. In Leslie's data there are the negative items *bedtime* and *ragtime*. That these do not have glottal realization can be explained by the non-overlapping syllabification in the underlying form, ie.

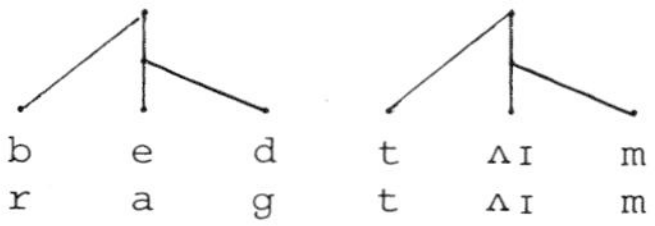
b e d t ʌɪ m
r a g t ʌɪ m

because English does not have any /-dt/ or /-gt/ clusters. *Sometime* [sʌmˀʌɪm] may be exceptional, though it depends whether *prompt* is /prɒmt/ or not. *Carlton* seems to be exceptional, too, with /-rlt/ in one syllable, but we must note that like all rhotic accents Edinburgh has final three-consonant clusters including /r/, eg. *world*, *words* and *pearls*.

[9]. The only other occurring sequences which fit the rule are /-lb/ in *bulb*, /-ldʒ/ in *bulge* and /-ndʒ/ in *change*. I have no evidence as to whether the /b/ would be deleted or not. In the plural form deletion would seem odd, but in rapid speech in an utterance such as *The bulb's gone* it might well take place. In my own rapid speech fricativization is more likely, i.e. [ðə bʌɬβz gɒn]. There is a tendency for the [d] to be deleted from /dʒ/, while the [ʒ] is retained, but again there are no instances in my recorded material.

[10]. With more data than I have used here it might be possible to show that certain processes are obligatory in certain styles, that is, equate the operation of particular rules with particular styles of delivery, interpreted by the native speaker as "formal", "casual", "posh", "common", and so on.

[11]. There are possible differences between informants C, B and W, which would involve adjustments to these rules in each case. Cf. Chapters 2 and 3, above.

[12]. I do not intend to pursue this point further here. For much fuller discussion of /ŋ/ in English

and German, see Goyvaerts (1978: 127-28) and Dressler (1981).

13. θ-harmony, as in *miss things* (cf. Lodge, 1981: 29), can be accounted for by rule 16, and θ-deletion, as in *sixth*, by applying Geminate Simplification afterwards. In *months* the order of the relevant segments is reversed and the rule would have to be revised to account for this too. NB: The examples containing [z] in Lodge (1981: 29-30) are incorrectly given a dental diacritic: [z̪].

14. For some interesting Celtic evidence, see Ó Dochartaigh (1980). For details of the change in Chinese, see Forrest (1973: 195).

15. I am not concerned here with whether we should take a metrical or a dependency view of syllable structure. Although there may be advantages to a dependency framework over a metrical one in terms of non-binarity and implicit strength values and structural levels that can be read off from the notation, I shall not attempt to argue the point here. On this and other matters, see Ewen (ms).

16. See Foley (1977: 123-26) for a discussion of "modular depotentiation" as his explanation for weakening of the strongest phonological elements. His treatment of English in this respect seems totally inadequate in terms of the data presented in this book.

17. For a discussion of /l/-deletion in Cockney and its relation to /r/-deletion, see Champ (1983). The former is not so widespread in the six accents discussed here as it is in Cockney.

149

REFERENCES

Aitchison, J. 1981. Language change: progress or decay? London: Fontana.

Aitken, A. J. 1962. Vowel length in Modern Scots. Mimeo: University of Edinburgh.

Anderson, J. M. ms. Suprasegmental structure. Paper presented at the Dependency Phonology Conference, University of Essex, 9-11 September 1983.

Anderson, J. M. and Ewen, C. J. 1980. Studies in dependency phonology. Ludwigsburg: Ludwigsburg Studies in Language and Linguistics 4.

Anderson, J. M. and Jones, C. 1977. Phonological structure and the history of English. Amsterdam: North-Holland.

Brown, G. 1972. Phonological rules and dialect variation. Cambridge: Cambridge University Press.

Brown, G. 1981. Consonant rounding in British English: the status of phonetic descriptions as historical data. In R. E. Asher and E. J. A. Henderson (eds.): Towards a history of phonetics. Edinburgh: Edinburgh University Press.

Champ, P. 1983. The evaporation of liquids in Cockney. Nottingham Linguistic Circular. 12.1: 1-20.

Cheshire, J. 1982. Linguistic variation and social function. In Romaine (1982).

Chomsky, A. N. 1980. Rules and representations. Oxford: Basil Blackwell.

Chomsky, A. N. and Halle, M. 1968. The sound pattern of English. New York: Harper and Row. (= SPE)

Cutler, A. 1980. Productivity in word formation. CLS. 16: 45-51.

Davenport, M. and Staun, J. ms. Some problems for dependency phonology. Paper presented at the Dependency Phonology Conference, University of Essex, 9-11 September 1983.

Dorian, N. C. 1982. Defining the speech community to include its working margins. In Romaine (1982).

Dresher, B. E. 1981. Abstractness and explanation in phonology. In N. Hornstein and D. Lightfoot (eds.): Explanation in linguistics. London: Longman.

Dressler, W. U. 1975. Methodisches zu Allegro-Regeln. In W. U. Dressler and F. V. Mareš (eds.): Phonologica 1972. Munich: Wilhelm Fink.

Dressler, W. U. 1981. External evidence for an

abstract analysis of the German velar nasal.
In D. L. Goyvaerts (ed.): Phonology in the 1980s.
Ghent: E. Story-Scientia.
Ewen, C. J. 1977. Aitken's law and the phonatory
gesture in dependency phonology. Lingua. 41:
307-29.
Ewen, C. J. 1980. Aspects of phonological structure.
Unpublished doctoral thesis, University of Edin-
burgh.
Ewen, C. J. ms. Segmental structure. Paper presen-
ted at the Dependency Phonology Conference,
University of Essex, 9-11 September 1983.
Ferguson, C. 1978. Phonological processes. In
J. H. Greenberg et al. (eds.): Universals of
human language. Stanford: Stanford University
Press.
Foley, J. 1970. Phonological distinctive features.
Folia Linguistica. 4: 87-92.
Foley, J. 1977. Foundations of theoretical phono-
logy. Cambridge: Cambridge University Press.
Forrest, R. A. D. 1973. The Chinese language.
(3rd ed.) London: Faber and Faber.
Fudge, E. C. 1967. The nature of phonological
primes. JL. 3: 1-36.
Fudge, E. C. 1969a. Mutation rules and ordering in
phonology. JL. 5: 23-38.
Fudge, E. C. 1969b. Syllables. JL. 5: 253-86.
Giles, H. and Powesland, P. F. 1975. Speech style
and social evaluation. London and New York:
Academic Press.
Gimson, A. C. 1962. An introduction to the pronun-
ciation of English. London: Edward Arnold.
Goldsmith, J. 1976a. Autosegmental phonology.
Bloomington: Indiana University Linguistics Club.
Goldsmith, J. 1976b. An overview of autosegmental
phonology. LA. 2: 23-68.
Goyvaerts, D. L. 1978. Aspects of post-SPE phono-
logy. Ghent: E. Story-Scientia.
Guy, G. 1980. Variation in the group and the indi-
vidual: the case of final stop deletion. In
Labov (1980).
Hardcastle, W. J. 1981. Experimental studies in
lingual coarticulation. In R. E. Asher and
E. J. A. Henderson (eds.): Towards a history of
phonetics. Edinburgh: Edinburgh University
Press.
Hasegawa, N. 1979. Casual speech vs. fast speech.
CLS. 15: 126-37.
Hockett, C. F. 1958. A course in modern linguistics.
New York: Macmillan.
Hooper, J. B. 1976. An introduction to natural

generative phonology. New York: Academic Press.
Hughes, A. and Trudgill, P. J. 1979. English accents
   and dialects. London: Edward Arnold.
Hyman, L. M. 1975. Phonology: theory and analysis.
   New York: Holt, Rinehart and Winston.
Kiparsky, P. 1968. How abstract is phonology?
   Bloomington: Indiana University Linguistics Club.
Kiparsky, P. 1979. Metrical structure assignment
   is cyclic. LI. 10: 421-41.
Knowles, G. 1978. The nature of phonological vari-
   ables in Scouse. In Trudgill (1978).
Labov, W. 1980. The social origins of sound change.
   In W. Labov (ed.): Locating language in time and
   space. New York: Academic Press.
Ladefoged, P. 1982. A course in phonetics. (2nd
   ed.) New York: Harcourt, Brace and Jovanovich.
Lass, R. 1976. English phonology and phonological
   theory. Cambridge: Cambridge University Press.
Leslie, D. ms. Left capture and British voiceless
   stop allophony. Paper presented at the XIX
   Congress of the International Association of
   Logopaedics and Phoniatrics, University of
   Edinburgh, 14-18 August 1983.
Liberman, M. and Prince, A. 1977. On stress and
   linguistic rhythm. LI. 8: 249-336.
Lodge, K. R. 1966. The Stockport dialect. Le
   maître phonétique. 126: 26-30.
Lodge, K. R. 1973. Stockport revisited. JIPA.
   3: 81-87.
Lodge, K. R. 1976. Some arguments concerning ideal-
   ization in linguistic descriptions. University
   of East Anglia Papers in Linguistics. 1: 1-14.
Lodge, K. R. 1978. A Stockport teenager. JIPA.
   8: 56-71.
Lodge, K. R. 1979. A three-dimensional analysis of
   non-standard English. Journal of Pragmatics.
   3: 169-195.
Lodge, K. R. 1981. Dependency phonology and English
   consonants. Lingua. 54: 19-39.
Lodge, K. R. 1983. The acquisition of phonology:
   a Stockport sample. Lingua.
Lodge, K. R. ms. The English velar fricative,
   dialect variation and dependency phonology.
   Paper presented at the Dependency Phonology
   Conference, University of Essex, 9-11 September
   1983.
Lodge, K. R. In preparation. Testing native speaker
   predictions of variant forms of English.
Lyons, J. 1962. Phonemic and non-phonemic phonology:
   some typological reflections. IJAL. 28: 131-58.

McEntegart, D. and Le Page, R. B. 1982. An appraisal
    of the statistical techniques used in the Socio-
    linguistic Survey of Multilingual Communities.
    In Romaine (1982).
Milroy, J. 1982. The tip of the iceberg. In
    Romaine (1982).
Milroy, J. and Milroy, L. 1978. Belfast: change
    and variation in an urban vernacular. In
    Trudgill (1978).
Milroy, L. 1980. Language and social networks.
    Oxford: Basil Blackwell.
Neu, H. 1980. Ranking of constraints on /t, d/
    deletion in American English: a statistical
    analysis. In Labov (1980).
Newton, B. 1970. Cypriot Greek, its phonology and
    inflections. The Hague: Mouton.
Ó Dochartaigh, C. 1980. Aspects of Celtic lenition.
    In Anderson and Ewen (1980).
Orton, H. et al. (eds.) 1962-71. Survey of English
    Dialects, Volumes I-IV. Leeds: Arnold. (= SED)
Palmer, F. R. (ed.) 1970. Prosodic analysis.
    London: Oxford University Press.
Petyt, K. M. 1978. Secondary contractions in West
    Yorkshire negatives. In Trudgill (1978).
Petyt, K. M. 1980. The study of dialect. London:
    André Deutsch.
Romaine, S. 1978. Postvocalic /r/ in Scottish
    English: sound change in progress? In Trudgill
    (1978).
Romaine, S. (ed.) 1982. Sociolinguistic variation
    in speech communities. London: Edward Arnold.
Sankoff, D. (ed.) 1978. Linguistic variation:
    models and methods. New York: Academic Press.
Selkirk, E. O. 1980. The role of prosodic categories
    in English word stress. LI. 11: 563-605.
Stampe, D. 1979. A dissertation on natural phonology.
    Including: The acquisition of phonetic represent-
    ation. Bloomington: Indiana University Linguist-
    ics Club.
Strang, B. M. H. 1970. A history of English.
    London: Methuen.
Tiersma, P. 1983. The nature of phonological repre-
    sentation: evidence from breaking in Frisian.
    JL. 19: 59-78.
Trager, G. L. and Smith H. L. 1951. An outline of
    English structure. Studies in Linguistics,
    Occasional Papers, 3. Norman, Oklahoma: Batten-
    burg Press.
Trudgill, P. J. 1974. The social differentiation of
    English in Norwich. Cambridge: Cambridge Univ-
    ersity Press.

Trudgill, P. J. 1978. Sociolinguistic patterns in British English. London: Edward Arnold.

Trudgill, P. J. 1980/83. Acts of conflicting identity. In Trudgill (1983).

Trudgill, P. J. 1983. On dialect. Oxford: Basil Blackwell.

Trudgill, P. J. 1983a. Sociolinguistics and linguistic theory. In Trudgill (1983).

Trudgill, P. J. and Foxcroft, T. 1978. On the sociolinguistics of vocalic mergers: transfer and approximation in East Anglia. In Trudgill (1978).

Vihman, M. M. 1978. Consonant harmony: its scope and function in child language. In J. H. Greenberg et al. (eds.) Universals of human language. Stanford: Stanford University Press.

Wells, J. C. 1982. Accents of English, Volumes 1 and 2. Cambridge: Cambridge University Press.

Zwicky, A. 1972. Casual speech. CLS. 8: 607-15.

INDEX

155

WORD INDEX

The word index contains forms which are discussed phonetically and/or phonologically in the text of the book. It does not contain references to the transcriptions, nor forms from the indented lists of examples in the various chapters. With four exceptions there are only one-word entries.